For "Marsl"
With best Wish

[signature]

DUNNINGER'S SECRETS

DUNNINGER'S SECRETS

by Dunninger

as told to
Walter Gibson

Lyle Stuart, Inc. • Secaucus, New Jersey

ONE

In this book, I have drawn upon my personal observations, recollections, and experiences over a period of nearly seventy-five years in the field of telepathy, or as I prefer to call it, thought-reading.

I first became aware of my ability in that direction at the age of seven, when I told my father the names of people who knocked at our door, before he opened it. These were strangers who introduced themselves when my father admitted them, so obviously they had their names in mind, which explained how I picked up the thought impressions. But it happened so frequently that my family began to think that it was uncanny, although to me it seemed both natural and normal.

About that time, my uncle took me to see Kellar, the famous magician, at the Academy of Music on Fourteenth Street, in New York. I was so intrigued with Kellar's wizardry that I made a decision, then and there, to become a magician in my own right. I spent so much time reading magic books and practicing new tricks that I neglected my schoolwork; but often, when the teacher gave the class a test, the right answers would spring to my mind spontaneously. Whether I was picking them up from the teacher's mind, or from the minds of the other scholars, I'm still not sure. I only know that the teacher watched me like a hawk, but never caught me cribbing from anybody else's papers.

After I finished school, I took various daytime jobs. In the evening, I put on magic shows, gradually working my fees upward, until it became more profitable to stay with magic entirely. One reason for my rapid success was that I varied my performances instead of limiting myself to one field. This enabled me to change my program and make new tours over the same vaudeville circuits, or give repeat shows at clubs and theaters where I had already appeared.

This was at variance with the usual pattern, as magicians of those days liked to specialize in certain fields. There were Card Kings, Coin Kings, Silk Kings, and Escape Kings. One performer even put on an entire act using only watches and clocks.

At that time, more than sixty years ago, I

advertised myself as an illusionist, but the term was highly inclusive. Magicians, themselves, used the term "illusion" to signify a large stage effect, such as the evanishment of an assistant from a cabinet or the levitation of a lady in midair. But, if you refer back to the unabridged dictionaries of that period, you will find an illusionist defined as "a producer of illusions, as a conjurer or prestidigitator."

That I was, in full-fledged form. I have always claimed that the size of the properties involved are unimportant in the production of a magical effect. A small, even trivial mystery can prove quite as astounding as a highly advertised, super sensation—sometimes even more so. Houdini proved that when he presented his "Vanishing Elephant" at the New York Hippodrome one season; while the next year, on the same huge stage, he performed the close-up feat of apparently swallowing a length of thread and a packet of needles, then bringing the thread from his mouth with the needles strung at intervals along it.

Actually, the "Needle Trick" was more of a mystery because it was performed with common, unprepared articles, whereas the elephant vanish required a huge, specially built cabinet. Similarly, the vaudeville sensation of "Sawing a Woman in Half," as introduced by Horace

Goldin, was more than matched by Cardini, the suave deceptionist who repeatedly plucked fans of playing cards from thin air, his act increasing in bafflement as he continued. The sole purpose is to make people think that they are witnessing the impossible. That's magic.

One of my early specialties was the "Chinese Linking Rings" in which as many as a dozen large steel rings are caused to link and unlink in bewildering fashion. Though very old, this effect is always new when capably presented. I will match my rendition of the "Linking Rings" against any other. Yet, at the same time, I give due credit to noted magicians of my era who worked masterful routines of their own. But as time went on, inferior sets of rings were peddled indiscriminately and even included in juvenile boxes of magic tricks. As a result, most professional magicians dropped the effect from their programs, but I updated my presentation by telling how the trick was commonly worked with only two genuinely single rings, the rest being faked or permanently linked. I then proceeded to demonstrate to everyone's satisfaction that every ring I used was single and separate at the start; that all could be linked together and separated as desired; and that any ring could be examined at any time by anyone.

I have cited this case to stress an important

point. In doing magic, you must make yourself believe that you are performing *real magic* in order to make it actually look so. That represents the gap between the Magic of the Masters and the Trickery of Today, a chasm so wide that some of the current would-be wizards are too shortsighted even to see it, and therefore don't even know that it is there.

Every great magician of the past impressed his personality upon his audience from the moment he strode on stage and built it more strongly as his program proceeded. There were differences in their styles: Some were bland, others genial. Some added a satanic touch to their artistry, while others adopted a courtly or gentlemanly pose. But always, they were magical to the tips of their deft fingers, and they shrouded themselves in an aura of mystery that bound the onlookers in its spell.

Contrast that with the modern tyro who ambles on stage, does a few quickies with a piece of rope or tears up a sheet of newspaper, folds it, and opens it intact, all the while beguiling his audience with an "I-told-you-so" smirk. After more such miracles, the spectators relax in relief as the performer bows off, but their respite is short-lived for then two half-trained assistants wheel an odd-shaped cabinet on stage and clumsily turn it about as though stalling for time, which they are. That becomes obvious when the performer returns wearing a garish uniform that looks as though it was designed for a lion tamer rather than a magician. With him, he brings a victim in the person of a young lady, who screams in terror when the magician cues his burly assistants to clamp her in the cabinet and close the doors.

Spikes, swords, and sheets of steel are then thrust through apertures designed to receive them. After that long and laborious process has been completed, it is repeated in reverse when the assistants remove the assorted hardware, and the cabinet is reopened to reveal the girl as undamaged as when she entered. Bows follow from the magician and his crew, leaving the spectators wondering, but not how the girl managed to keep clear of the pointed implements, for obviously, she knew where each was due. Their real wonder is why the magician, if he really wanted to destroy the girl, didn't simply plant a time bomb in the cabinet. It certainly would have been there long enough to have gone off, even with an oversized fuse.

Contraptions of this type are termed "torture illusions," and the title is well chosen, but it is the audience who suffers, not the young lady who is supposed to be undergoing an ordeal. The same applies to a whole catalog full of

magical contrivances ranging in size from rabbit boxes to those designed for human beings,
who can be vanished or produced in almost any
fashion except mysteriously, since the audience
invariably knows what to expect.

This "horrible" example simply shows what
can happen to any form of artistry when it is
reduced to a push-button process. Where magic
is concerned, I saw it coming before most of the
bunglers who are now ruining it were even
born, so I can hold no grudge against them.
They didn't have the privilege of witnessing the
inimitable performances of Herrmann the
Great, as such later greats as Thurston and
Raymond did. Nor were they inspired by the
baffling deceptions of the Great Kellar, as Houdini and I were.

Fake spirit mediums were rampant in Kellar's
day, so he put on a spirit cabinet act that made
them look like apprentices. Today, it is laugh-
able when self-styled authorities on psychic
subjects become effusive over old-time mediums like the Davenport Brothers who produced
spooky manifestations while tightly roped inside a big cabinet with double doors. In the next
breath, those same authorities will say that any
spirit effects produced by stage magicians are
just "tricks" and nothing more.

It might surprise them to learn that Kellar, in

his early days, worked with William Fay, who had managed the Davenports during their prime and that Kellar's cabinet was patterned on the one the brothers had used. Moreover, Kellar's rope tie, which he performed in full view of the audience, was one that he had learned from Fay and had improved far beyond the method used by the Davenports. Where mediums could cause a table to tilt by pressing their hands against the edge, Kellar would place one hand squarely on the top and raise the table completely in midair while standing on a fully lighted stage.

Kellar's mastery of the miraculous was not confined to spirit phenomena. His famous flower growth, in which he caused two full-sized rose bushes to appear in pots placed beneath two empty cones, became more baffling every time you witnessed it. Even magicians who performed the flower growth themselves were mystified by Kellar's method, so great was his ability to divert an entire audience's attention at the crucial moment. Magicians term this "misdirection," and they all practice it to some degree, but often in a stylized or almost-obvious manner. That, however, was not the case with Kellar. There was something actually hypnotic in his manner. I was always eager to talk with Kellar and learn his views on the subject.

My chance came after Kellar retired from the

12

stage and designated Howard Thurston as his successor. For a while, Kellar lived in New York City and frequently visited Martinka's Magic Shop at 493 Sixth Avenue, which was then a mecca for magi. Later, Martinka's merged with the Hornmann Magic Company at 304 West Thirty-fourth Street, which is still owned and managed by my lifelong friend Al Flosso and his son Jack. But in those old, old days, it was still in the shadow of the Sixth Avenue elevated subway, and that was where I first met Kellar, who after his retirement became one of the most amiable men in his profession, always glad to encourage aspiring newcomers.

I told Kellar that I had heard someone quote him as saying that if he could gain the full attention of an audience, a brass band could march across the stage in back of him, playing at full blast, with a herd of elephants following, yet no one would know that the parade had gone by. I can still see the twinkle in his eye as he acknowledged that he had made an extravagant claim of that sort during a newspaper interview; but his tone turned serious when he added that it not only could happen with some people, actually, it could go much farther.

As Kellar put it: "All magicians know that the more your mind is fixed on one thing, the easier it is to miss something else. So if you miss anything, you are not to blame. It only means that you have a mind of your own. But when you see things that aren't there, that's different."

I was prompt to ask, "You mean people imagining that they saw ghosts in your spirit cabinet?"

"No, no." Kellar shook his head at that. "They saw dummy forms that looked like ghosts, so it was easy for anyone who believed in ghosts to mistake them for the real thing. I was speaking about my devils."

Briefly, I was puzzled. Then I remembered Kellar's billboard advertising, those flamboyant lithographs that ran the gamut from one-sheets to twenty-fours. Many had a common feature that was practically a trademark. When Kellar was depicted performing a large illusion, a life-size figure of Mephistopheles would be standing in the background, looking on approvingly. When Kellar was working intermediate effects, lesser demons would be seated near the footlights, delving into mysterious books, as though looking for helpful incantations. Even in a close-up portrait, Kellar was apt to have an imp perching on his shoulder, whispering in his ear.

"So people came to the show expecting to see devils," I remarked. "When they didn't see them, they must have been disappointed—"

"It was just the other way about," put in

Kellar. "The people who came to the show expecting to see devils generally did see them, or thought they did. All over the stage and even in the theater lobby, when they were on the way out."

Kellar went on to recall specific cases that he had encountered in his travels, not just in faraway lands, where belief in devils might be expected, but in many American cities where I hoped someday to play the leading theaters with my own big magic show. When I thought it over, the more impressed I became with the way Kellar had preconditioned his audiences to accept the incredible. While I did not have the advantage of such advance billing, I still could see a way whereby I could work on the susceptibilities of individuals in an audience and thus create a stronger impression on the rest.

In trying to develop all phases related to magic, I had delved deeply into hypnotism, which at that time was increasing rapidly in popularity. However, to put on a bona fide hypnotic act was practically impossible for several reasons. First, many of the best subjects in the average audience were reluctant to come up on the platform and make a show of themselves; while to hypnotize those who did come up could prove to be a lengthy process, too slow to hold the interest of the crowd. So most hypnotists simply put on a well-faked show, using gags of a hypnotic type with the average volunteer and depending on stooges for the more spectacular tests.

Not that the hypnotic acts weren't good. Too often, they were too good, because very few spectators could distinguish the real from the fake. The stooges who came up from the audience weren't merely local yokels who went through a rehearsed routine. They were specialists who traveled along with the show and were known as "horses" to the trade. A good horse would let his lips be sewn together with needle and thread and would allow skewers to be thrust through the fleshy part of his arms, throat, and cheeks. A horse would go rigid at the hypnotist's command so he could lie stretched between two chairs while three men sat on his body.

All that hokum threatened to put hypnotic acts back in the dime museums from which they had emerged. Since I had set my sights on something bigger and better, I was ready to cross hypnotism off the list, until Kellar's experience rang home. I realized that people who believed they would see the devils depicted in Kellar's posters were practically self-hypnotized when they came into the theater. As a result, when Kellar presented the illusions shown on the billboards, they became so real, that they thought they saw the devils, too. This was a definitive case of posthypnosis, in which an impression, once implanted hypnotically, becomes recurrent.

Since my audiences were smaller and more intimate than Kellar's, I decided to use that sort of hypnotism as an adjunct to my magic. From that day on, when I went down into the audience to pass articles for examination, I no longer picked the nearest spectator or picked somebody at random. I looked for a good hypnotic subject, one who would respond to whatever suggestion I had in mind. Moreover, I was choosy, often passing by a few good candidates in order to note their reactions. Those who froze indignantly, I ignored. Others, who felt eager to be noticed, I reserved for greater purposes. When I invited volunteers to come up on the stage, I looked directly at those chosen few. And believe me, they would come up so fast and so eagerly, that I began to understand how effectively telepathy works, though frankly, I hadn't given it very serious thought until then—and still didn't for a while.

I had an advantage over Kellar, who had to go by the reports that were relayed back to him. In my case, I could tell from the audience reactions just how well I was doing with my handpicked subjects. Also, since I played repeat engagements, I was constantly hearing reports of wonders that I had performed—some were so extravagant that I began wondering if I had really performed them. Some of these, I could track down. For instance, the man who practically swore an oath that I had handed him two solid steel rings which he had linked together and then unlinked without realizing how it could have happened. Naturally, he couldn't have realized it, because it couldn't have happened. What must have happened was this:

I said, "Take these two rings and try to put them together." Then, as he faltered, I added, helpfully, "Just let me show you how. You hold them like this"—which he started to do—"and you twist them like this"—which I showed him how—"and when you hold them like this"—which he was doing by then—"you will find that they are solidly linked together"—which they were! But when he insisted that he had unlinked them, he was wrong. He couldn't have.

That was when I said, even more helpfully, "Would you like to see how easy it is to unlink them? Just let me give them to the gentleman over here"—which I did—"and he will find that they are unlinked." Which they were. Whereupon, I turned to the first man, my original hypnotic subject, and said, "You see, you linked them and you unlinked them." To which he totally agreed, though actually, he had done neither. When I met him twenty years later, he still bragged that he was the man who had linked and unlinked a pair of rings without my even touching them.

I went along with that, for two good reasons. First, because he insisted that it was my magic that had been responsible; and second, because I was glad to know that a posthypnotic impression could last that long. More vital was the fact that I had been using that power of suggestion through all those years, with highly profitable results. Instead of confining it to standard routines like the Linking Rings, I applied it to mental effects as well. It reminded me of my old school days, when the teacher would ask a question and try to pick the only scholar who didn't have the answer, which was usually me. Only the teacher never realized that either she was projecting the answer mentally, or that I was picking it up from other students who were eagerly waving their hands because they already had the answer. During my act, I was either projecting thoughts to minds that I sensed were receptive, like my own; or I was picking up impressions that they wanted me to gain.

All that came under the general head of what is loosely termed "hypnotic clairvoyance," which is as old as hypnotism itself. Questions put to ancient oracles were answered by sibyls who were in a trance state. Belief in oracles persisted on through the Middle Ages, until, just two centuries ago, a Viennese physician, Franz Anton Mesmer, propounded a theory of animal magnetism that became the basis of modern hypnotism. Almost from the start, Mesmer found that he could establish what he termed a *rapport* with some of his more responsive subjects. During that state, they would obey his unspoken commands. That was the essence of hypnotic clairvoyance.

Hypnotism has come a long way since Mesmer's time. It was discredited, then rediscovered, and finally given scientific status. As a result, new terms have come into vogue, such as cryptesthesia, to denote an "all-inclusive psychic sense"; telesthesia, which is limited to "impressions received at a distance"; telepathy, defined as actual "thought transmission"; and even hyperesthesia, or a "highly extreme sensitivity of the normal senses." All these can be grouped under the general head of ESP, or extrasensory perception, which is the most modern term of all. Yet it is still practically a flashback to the old clairvoyant faculty with its hypnotic overtones.

DUNNINGER'S SECRETS

Innumerable cases could be cited of persons who have displayed this faculty since Mesmer's time. One standout of more than a century ago, was a Parisian youth named Alexis Didier, who could describe hidden objects and distant scenes with uncanny facility while in a hypnotic trance. Alexis was tested and declared genuine by the famous French magician, Robert-Houdin, whose name was later appropriated by Houdini.

A more modern instance is that of Edgar Cayce, who correctly diagnosed hundreds of baffling medical cases and prescribed the proper remedies while in a hypnotic trance. I personally have used hypnotism under medical supervision to cure cases of stammering and hiccups; and I have also done clinical work in which I relieved the pain of patients through hypnotism when the administration of narcotics was inadvisable.

But my prime interest, of course, has been in the entertainment field, where I have gained results far beyond any of my predecessors. One of my first achievements was to improve a test made famous by a mentalist named Washington Irving Bishop, nearly a century ago. Bishop would have someone concentrate on the serial number of a bank note; then, holding the person's arm, he would proceed to write the entire number, figure by figure, on a blackboard.

This was a very convincing test, which Bishop presented almost without a flaw, provided, of course, that the person kept thinking of each figure in its proper order, as it was definitely an experiment in thought-reading.

Skeptics claimed that Bishop picked up the figures through muscular impulses, though it would have been difficult indeed for him to do so with such continued success. However, to disprove that claim, I revived the bank note test and developed it to such perfection that I can call off an entire number without any contact whatever. Though, in some cases, I have the person hold the other end of a shoestring in order to concentrate effectively, but the string is always allowed to dangle loosely.

One time a critic took exception to my "number test" because I referred to a bill that a woman was holding as a "dollar bill," when it happened to be a ten. The critic argued that if I really was a mind reader, I should have known and stated the denomination of the bill. That is the sort of stupidity I sometimes encountered.

I had told the woman to memorize the number on a bill and she had asked, "A dollar bill?" To which I replied, "Yes, any dollar bill—or any bill." The fact that she had decided to use a ten dollar bill without saying so had no bearing whatever on the test, as I was concentrating solely on the serial number. The fact that I named every figure correctly was apparently something that the critic wanted to dodge, since he had absolutely no way of explaining how I could have accomplished it, except through telepathy. And that was something he didn't want to admit.

In contrast, I have always welcomed any type of byplay that added zest to a test. One time, after I had read the numbers correctly from three different bills, a genial spectator thrust his fist up in the air and announced, "I'm holding a dollar here in my hand, so let's see if you can call off the figures—right now."

That wasn't a new challenge. Often, someone would cup his hands around a bill so that I couldn't see it while he was memorizing the serial number, so I simply asked, "Are you sure you have memorized the number correctly?" He said, "Absolutely." I approached him, placed the fingertips of one hand on his fist and the fingertips of my other hand on my forehead.

"Think of each figure slowly," I told him. "I'm getting them now. One—nine—one—three—"

From the gleam in his eye and his half smile, I felt sure that I was right, but for some reason, I was stopped cold. It couldn't be that he was holding back on the rest, for his manner hadn't changed, unless he was showing a trace of

23

satisfaction at having stumped the Great Dunninger. That was when I stopped probing for the figures and tried to rationalize the situation. Then suddenly, the answer hit me.

"The figures on your dollar are one, nine, one, three," I repeated, "and that's all there are. They aren't part of a serial number, because you are holding a silver dollar, with the date nineteen hundred and thirteen. Let's see it."

He opened his hand and showed the silver dollar. I took it and passed it to another spectator who checked the date and found that it was 1913, exactly as I said.

Another test I introduced was to have three persons each think of a number of three figures and keep them constantly in mind. I would then write something in chalk on a large slate, which I rested on a chair, with the blank side of the slate toward the audience. I would then have the three persons write their numbers on a smaller slate—say 338, 676, 412—so that someone could add them, making the total 1,426. When I turned the big slate around for all to see, there was the answer: 1,426.

Magicians tried to imitate that test by switching the column of numbers for a set of their own, but they fizzled badly, because they couldn't check back the figures with the people who originally wrote them, as the total would be

wrong. In my presentation, the original numbers added up to the right total, for a very
simple reason. I was practically doing the serial
number test, but instead of having one man
think of eight figures, I had three people think
of three each, so I could add them mentally.
There was more risk, of course, because if I had
trouble with one person's number, it would
throw the others out of line. But I always chose
my subjects carefully for that test.

On one occasion, I invited a committee of
celebrities up on the stage of the New York
Hippodrome, and I picked a burly, carefree
individual as one of the men for the test. When I
asked him to think of a three figure number, I
had about the fastest mental flash I had ever
experienced, but it wasn't right.

Apologetically, I told him, "I'm sorry, but I
can't use you in this test. I asked for a number
with three figures, but all you have on your
mind is a two figure number. In fact, it's so
much on your mind, you can't think of anything
else. You practically shouted it at me mentally,
so I'll tell you what it was—the number sixty."

Immediately, the whole place rocked with
laughter and applause, leaving me totally nonplussed. While the din continued, I managed to
nudge a committeeman who was standing by
and ask him what it was all about. He blinked

and asked, "Don't you know who that is?"
When I shook my head, he told me, "That's
Babe Ruth, the home-run king with the New
York Yankees. Tonight, we were expecting him
to announce that he will be going after an all-
time record of sixty home runs this season, only
you beat him to it."

Next, the Babe himself was slapping me on
the back and giving me a powerful handclasp,
as he acknowledged, "You were right, Dunninger. When you asked for a number, I was ready
to shout 'Sixty!' like you said. But if you are that
good at reading minds, how about making a
prediction? Am I going to hit those sixty home
runs?"

Looking squarely at the mighty Babe Ruth, I
played a solid hunch.

"You're going to hit exactly sixty. Not one
more and not one less."

"Hear that?" Ruth turned to the group around
us. "I'm going to make it right on the button.
Dunninger says so. He's the man who knows
everything. So if I don't deliver, blame him, not
me."

The next day's headlines had me labeled as
the prophet of the year, which was a big order in
its own right; but what I had to avoid were
interviews by sports writers who wanted to
know if there was a system behind my predic-

tion. The fact was, I wouldn't have known a home run if I'd seen one, because I'd never seen a baseball game in my life and never intended to watch one.

At that time I was living in the Bronx and drove my car down to Manhattan nearly every day, always giving Yankee Stadium the widest possible detour to avoid the traffic there. But by the season's end, I had my innings, as I understand they say in baseball. Either my power of suggestion or the power of Ruth's bat produced the precise result I had predicted, exactly sixty home runs. Let some of today's self-appointed "prophets" match that if they can.

Through the years, I learned that the more intelligent and distinguished the audience, the more my demonstrations were appreciated. When King Edward VIII visited America as the Prince of Wales, I appeared at a special function given in his honor, and I was greatly impressed by his interest and cordiality. In my slate test, I usually had someone mark the blank side to make sure that the same slate was used throughout. So I offered His Royal Highness a piece of chalk and asked him if he would place his initials on the slate. To which he replied, whimsically, "That won't be necessary. I am sure everyone here knows who I am."

I might mention here that the prince, like his

grandfather, King Edward VII, was a skillful
amateur conjurer. He was subtly letting me
know that if any trickery was involved, he
would not only be capable of detecting it, but
would keep it to himself, as a fellow member of
the craft. I met him in later years after he
became Duke of Windsor, and he was prompt to
recall the incident.

When I appeared at a lavish party given for
Barbara Hutton, the Woolworth heiress, on the
important occasion of her twenty-first birthday,
she was extremely hopeful that I could repeat a
quotation that she had in mind. She concentrated on it very seriously and was pleased indeed
when I delivered it word for word: "If you have
two loaves of bread, sell one and buy a lily." A
very pretty thought, I felt, and highly appropriate for the occasion, with a philosophical touch
that should not be overlooked.

In all, I have entertained six presidents of the
United States, and I can recall highlights from
each engagement. My demonstrations did not
occur, however, while all were actually in office.
Some were before; others after, so it is best to
consider them in chronological order. Theodore
Roosevelt was the first—that was when I was an
aspiring young performer, so he probably
would not have remembered it as vividly as I
did.

DUNNINGER'S SECRETS

The next, strangely, was Warren G. Harding, while he was a senator. He was so impressed with my demonstration that I gave him a confidential prediction that he would become president of the United States, which I am sure that he didn't believe at the time. He probably didn't think that I did either, though I wouldn't have made such a forecast unless I had felt sure that it would be fulfilled.

William H. Taft was third, at a special event at the Hotel Astor, in New York. This was quite a few years after he had served as president, and not only was he genial as usual, he amiably challenged me to read the numbers on some bonds that he happened to have in his pocket. This, of course, was similar to my usual bill test, though the numbers varied in length, which meant that I had to know exactly when to stop, which I did. But give the credit to ex-President Taft and not to me. His mind was easy to read, one of the easiest I ever encountered. Perhaps that was why he retired so completely from the political scene.

I performed for Calvin Coolidge at the White House while he was president, and I found it rather a routine session. Coolidge had a flabby handshake and preferred to sit back and watch the proceedings rather than participate. In short, he was his usual silent self throughout, but I could tell that he was impressed by the

29

answers I gave to other people's questions.

Herbert Hoover was just the opposite when I appeared at the White House during his term of office. He concentrated upon a single thought and was quite amazed when I spelled it out, letter by letter: H-U-L-D-A—which happened to be his mother's name.

During the Roosevelt administration, I appeared at the White House three times and on one occasion, FDR asked me to name a number that he had in mind. I gave it correctly and added that it was a street address, though he had not specified that at the start. When he smilingly asked if I could name the street, I said that it was Pennsylvania Avenue and that it was the number of the White House itself, or at least the number which would normally have been given to the White House. I was correct in every detail, because the president had them all in mind; whereas in many instances, people only project partial thoughts, hence I am limited to picking up those impressions.

Eleanor Roosevelt was present on that occasion and became so enthusiastic over my program that she gave it special mention in her daily column. I met her at other functions later and found that her interest in my work was as keen as ever.

Another noted columnist whom I impressed

was O.O. McIntyre, whose *New York Day by Day* was widely read throughout the country. His comment is worth quoting here, as it summarizes my demonstration quite succinctly.

It ran as follows:

> My wife wrote "Who is K.G. and where born?" Nothing else. After writing the question secretively, she placed it in a vanity case. No one came near. The mystic suddenly exclaimed: "K.G. is Kate Greenwood. Your mother's maiden name. She was born May 1, 1854, in Gallipolis, Ohio." The answer was so absolutely correct, I spent the rest of the evening peeking under chairs. Fifty questions were so answered.

Despite so glowing a send-off from such a competent critic, there are still some skeptics who can't quite believe that such things can happen. They are more than counterbalanced, however, by others who will believe in almost anything. Those claims, pro and con, will be examined in the chapters that follow.

TWO

As I mentioned earlier, thought projection and its reception first came to the fore in the time of Franz Anton Mesmer, some two hundred years ago. Mesmer might be styled the Sigmund Freud of his day—or vice versa—for he explored the hidden channels of the mind and came up with some conclusions that were highly controversial, but far reaching in their results.

Both Mesmer and Freud were deeply interested in telepathic phenomena, but Mesmer, as a pioneer in the field, regarded it as a by-product of his "animal magnetism." He developed this theory from experiments with actual magnets that were attached to a patient's body in the hope that a magnetic flow would cure hysteria, convulsions, hallucinations, and a variety of nervous disorders. That, at the time, was by no means fanciful, for magnets were still something of a mystery, and new discoveries regarding electricity offered a connecting link.

From Mesmer's own accounts, he obviously recognized that his actions and his treatments were playing upon the imagination of his patients and that their confidence in him was another factor in their cures, but that caused him to advance new claims for the magnetic theory, which he expressed in these terms:

> I have found that steel is not the only object which can absorb and emanate a magnetic force. On the contrary, paper, bread, wood, silk, leather, stone, glass, water, various metals, dogs, human beings, everything which I touched, became so magnetic that these objects exerted as great an influence on the sick as does the magnet itself. I filled bottles with magnetic material, just as one does with electricity. I found two ways of intensifying this magnetic force to such an extent that, instead of feeling the agonizing pains, which last a long time, the patient felt spasms which followed each other in quick succession.

In Paris, where he created a huge sensation, Mesmer magnetized his patients in groups by seating them around a huge tub called a *baquet,*

DUNNINGER'S SECRETS

filled with stacked bottles of magnetized water.
Rods ran to the members of the group, who sat
with joined hands so that the magnetic current
could run freely about the circle. Mesmer
moved among them, touching them with his
hands or making magnetic passes so that they
could virtually feel or see the current flowing
from his fingertips.

That could be attributed to imagination on
their part, but Mesmer found that some of his
subjects were so susceptible that they would
obey his unspoken commands. In short, he
could induce what he termed a "crisis" wherein
a patient became convulsive, simply by "willing" it to happen. In accordance with his theory
that various objects could absorb and emanate a
magnetic force, Mesmer magnetized a tree and
had people gather about it like the *baquet*, with
the same convulsive results. Naturally, they
were responding to the power of suggestion,
which at that time was unlabeled as such.

During his rise to fame, Mesmer trained
others in his methods, among them a prominent
Parisian physician, Charles D'Eslon, who was
called upon to demonstrate animal magnetism
before a royal commission appointed to investi-
gate the current rage. Benjamin Franklin, who
was then in Paris, was a member of the commission, which convened in his garden. There

34

D'Eslon volunteered to duplicate Mesmer's test of magnetizing a tree to prove its power of attracting human beings.

The committee picked one of several small apricot trees, and D'Eslon magnetized it in Mesmer's best style. Then, he brought in his subject, a twelve-year-old boy who was so susceptible to magnetism that he should have wandered around Uncle Benny's garden and gone utterly convulsive when he came within range of the chosen apricot tree. Only it didn't happen.

Why not?

Because they brought the boy into the garden *wearing a blindfold.* What the boy did, was go into convulsions immediately, for the simple reason that he knew he should go into convulsions when the right time came. If he had been unblindfolded, which is an odd way to put it, yet correct, he would probably have waited until he came to the proper apricot tree.

But then, the committee would have claimed that D'Eslon had cued the boy and that the whole thing was a trick. It was to avoid that very situation that D'Eslon had either agreed upon the blindfold, or, indeed, may have insisted that it be used. Either way, it ruined his case completely.

The commission dismissed the magnetic

theory and charged the whole thing to "suggestibility," which it was; but they had no idea how far suggestibility could carry. What they proved conclusively was that Mesmer's "magnetism" certainly could not permeate wood, as he claimed, but a full understanding of its principles failed utterly to penetrate their own thick heads, which were closely akin to that substance. Otherwise, they would have recognized that D'Eslon's own sincere effort to prove his theories by blindfolding the boy had been the cause of his failure.

Always, scientific investigation into the field of mental phenomena has followed that same pattern, as we shall duly see. Conditions are imposed that handicap the demonstrations to a degree where success is all but impossible, and skeptics are quick to shout "fraud" at the slightest provocation. In contrast, where trickery is really involved, a smart operator can always outguess the doubters by first figuring ways to beat the conditions he anticipates and then insisting upon them himself. This was especially true in the case of the "Blindfold Test," which came into vogue immediately after D'Eslon's failure and has been a standby ever since.

In Paris, at that period, was a man known as Chevalier Pinetti, who advertised himself as a "professor of natural magic" and put on exhibitions of sleight of hand, mechanical figures, and other wonders. He even escaped from chains and locks, a century before Houdini became famous in that line. Pinetti appeared before the royal court and knew all about the commission that investigated D'Eslon and the failure that had followed. So Pinetti blandly put on an act of his own, first in Paris, then in London. I quote from a copy of a newspaper ad in the *London Post* of Dec. 1, 1784:

At the Theatre-Royal in the
HAY-MARKET
Tomorrow, December 2,
Signor Pinetti, Knight of the Order of Merit of St. Philip, &c., &c.,..... will exhibit most wonderful, stupendous and absolutely inimitable mechanical, physical and philosophical pieces ... among which Signorina Pinetti will have the special honour and satisfaction of exhibiting various experiments of new discovery, no less curious than seemingly incredible, particularly that of her being seated in one of the front boxes with a handkerchief over her eyes, and guess at every thing imagined and proposed to her, by any person in the company.

Among the things that Signorina Pinetti "guessed at"—I use quotes, because, believe me, she didn't have to guess!—were the names of playing cards taken from a shuffled pack. In those days, only a comparatively few people played cards and those who did were fairly poor shufflers. So to prove that the pack was well shuffled, Signor Pinetti shuffled it himself. That roused the skepticism of a Parisian journalist named Decremps, who explained it all in a book, entitled *La Magie Blanche Devoille* (*White Magic Unveiled*).

According to Decremps, Pinetti used a stacked deck which he apparently shuffled by giving it a series of rapid single cuts, which did not disturb the arrangement—or more correctly, the rotation—of the cards. After the signorina was blindfolded, Pinetti spread the deck and allowed a spectator to take a clump of cards from any place he wanted. By simply cutting the pack at that point and noting the bottom card, Pinetti learned the card that followed, which was the first card in the spectator's batch.

Here, as Decremps put it, "He says that he will not speak at all while the woman will name the cards and that the person who has drawn them must show them to the audience without adding that the woman has named such and such a card correctly. It is in that last sentence that he cleverly names the card that is on the bottom of the pack. The woman who hears it also knows the arrangement and thereby names the cards that follow. For example, if the performer lets her know that the fifteenth card is on the bottom, she names the sixteenth, seventeenth, etc."

At that point, Pinetti injected a neat touch by having the spectator shuffle or mix the cards he drew before spreading them in a fan toward himself, so that each time the woman named a card, he could pick it from the fan and show it. He then replaced it. This served two purposes. First, though the woman actually named the cards in order, she apparently called them haphazardly. Second, since the spectator alone kept track of the cards, there was presumably no way for either the performer or the woman to know when all had been called.

However, all Pinetti had to do was slip the top card of the pack to the bottom and casually note it, thereby learning where the sequence ended. So when the signorina came to the card just before it, Pinetti, as if to speed the action, would say to the spectator, "Tell her to name some more." That was the cue for the signorina to ponder and finally come up with the exclamation, "But there are no more!"

Simple though this sounds, it is so good that

would-be mentalists have been reinventing it with slight embellishments ever since Pinetti's time. In fact, many performers still use a system of prearrangement published nearly a century ago, which is easily remembered by the following verse, that suggests the values of the cards in a fixed order:

Eight kings threatened to save
8   king   3   10   2   7

Ninety-five ladies for one sick knave
9   5   queen   4   ace   6   jack

Suits also follow a regular order of diamonds, clubs, hearts, spades, which can be remembered by the word DuCHeSs. So the pack, starting from the top, would run 8 D, K C, 3 H, 10 S, 2 D, 7 C, 9 H, 5 S, Q D, 4 C, A H, 6 S, J D, 8 C, K H, 3 S, 10 D, 2 C, 7 H, 9 S, 5 D, Q C, 4 H, A S, 6 D, J C, 8 H, K S, 3 D, 10 C, 2 H, 7 S, 9 D, 5 C, Q H, 4 S, A D, 6 C, J H, 8 S, K D, 3 C, 10 H, 2 S, 7 D, 9 C, 5 H, Q S, 4 D, A C, 6 H, J S.

If Pinetti had been using that particular setup, he might have noted the queen of hearts as his bottom card, after the spectator had taken a batch from the pack. In that case, he would have told the spectator, "I will not speak at all and neither should you. If the signorina should name a card correctly, such as the queen of hearts, don't say anything; just show the card to the audience and wait for her to name another. Let the cards speak for themselves by showing them."

Since the queen of hearts wasn't in the batch that the spectator took, everyone would have assumed that Pinetti cited it just as an example. That is, everyone except the signorina, who took that card as her cue to name the four of spades, ace of diamonds, six of clubs, and so on in deliberate succession, giving the astounded spectator time to find and show each card to the equally amazed audience. Meanwhile, Pinetti was checking the top card of the pack—say the two of spades—so when the signorina announced, "ten of hearts," he followed with the comment, "Tell her to name some more," and that finished it.

Not that Pinetti always cued the signorina that boldly. Elsewhere in his book, Decremps credits Pinetti with transmitting the name of a card by "asking a question in which the first syllables or the last vowels of the words give the assistant the color and value of the card." The same applied to the numbers on dice rolled by a spectator and the names of various objects which were shown to the audience and called off by the blindfolded lady.

41

Despite Decremps' explanation, Pinetti continued to baffle audiences with his "second-
sight" act, proving conclusively that a good
performer has no need to worry over so-called
"exposures" of his methods, a rule that has held
true ever since. In fact, it is doubtful that
Decremps ever did catch on to Pinetti's code or
he would have spelled it out in detail. So if it
was that good, it was no wonder Pinetti held his
public. More than half a century later, the
second-sight act cropped up as a new sensation,
when an eight-year-old Scottish boy, Louis
Gordon M'Kean appeared in London and demonstrated his ability to name the dates on coins
and describe various articles while blindfolded.

That was in 1831 and as M'Kean grew older,
he took his younger brothers into the act. Either
some of the M'Kean family or a new troupe were
still doing business as late as 1850, when P.T.
Barnum brought them back from England to
appear at his famous museum in New York. It
was Barnum who gave the first fully detailed
explanation of the code used in such acts. It
appeared in his autobiography as follows:

The Scotch boys were interesting for
the mysterious method by which one of
them, though blindfolded, answered
questions put by the other respecting

objects presented by persons who attended the surprising exhibition. The mystery, which was merely the result of patient practice, consisted wholly in the manner in which the question was propounded; in fact, the question invariably carried its own answer; for instance:

"What is this?" meant gold; "Now what is this?" silver; "Say what is this?" copper; "Tell me what is this?" iron; "What is the shape?" long; "Now what shape?" round; "Say what shape," square; "Please say what this is," a watch; "Can you tell what is in this lady's hand?" a purse; "Now please say what this is," a key; "Come now, what is this?" money; "How much?" a penny; "Now how much?" sixpence; "Say how much," a quarter of a dollar; "What color is this?" black; "Now what color is this?" red; "Say what color," green; and so on, ad infinitum. To such perfection was this brought that it was almost impossible to present any object that could not be quite closely described by the blindfolded boy. This is the key to all exhibitions of what is called "second sight."

Barnum first published his autobiography in 1869 and kept adding to it in new editions up until his death in 1891. He offered it at special prices at his museums, with his circuses, and by mail order, so that in those twenty-odd years, he sold or gave away more than a million copies, all explaining the "second-sight" act as described above.

Yet when Houdini started on the road as a youthful magician, in 1894, he and his wife Bessie featured the very same old second sight, using the same type of code that the majority of the million readers of Barnum's book should have recognized immediately after the act began.

Their code consisted of ten "key words" representing figures as follows:

Pray—1   Please—6
Answer—2   Speak—7
Say—3   Quickly—8
Now—4   Look—9
Tell—5   Be quick—0

Check this list against Barnum's examples, and you will find that the Houdinis were using four key words that dated back to the Scotch boys: "now," "say," "tell," and "please." Evidently "come" and "can" (or "can you") were on the Scotch boys' list; and they also registered a figure by simply asking "what" or "how much" without using a special key word. So the gaff was "old hat" when the Houdinis began using it. Yet after Houdini's death in 1926, Bessie revealed their "spoken code words" as something that had been "kept secret for thirty-three years."

This simply goes to prove that Barnum was right when he made his famous statement that "There's a sucker born every minute." That certainly applied to any of the buyers of Barnum's book who happened to witness the mind reading act that the Houdinis were putting on in circuses and sideshows, the very sort of places where those buyers were apt to go. But the fact is, the act itself was a real fooler and still is today. Houdini gave it up early in order to specialize in escapes from handcuffs and other restraints. But while he was finding fame the hard way, other vaudeville teams—the Zancigs, the Ushers, the Zomahs, to mention just a few— found not only fame but fortune by building the old code-act up to the point where it bordered on the miraculous.

In preparing for the act, the two members of the team memorize lists of objects, colors, names of persons, countries, states, cities, and so on. This takes time, but it is worth it and by

DUNNINGER'S SECRETS

using a regular memory system, these lists can be extended to a hundred items each, though some—like colors—only need a dozen or so. Usually, as with the Houdinis, the man works the audience while the woman, seated on the platform or stage, acts as the medium.

Suppose the man is handed a locket and it happens to be number forty-six on the list of objects. He would say, "Now please name this object," thus coding "4" (now) and "6" (please), which to the medium would mean "46." If the locket had a chain attached, with fifty-eight being the number for it, the man would continue, "Tell me what this is. Quickly." That would register as "5" (tell) and "8" (quickly) thus signifying fifty-eight. With first names of people, two lists are frequently used, one for men, the other for women. Thus, "Please say what this man's name is," would be "4" (please) and "3" (say) which could stand for "James" as forty-three on the men's list. While, "This lady's name—speak up and answer!" would be "7" (speak) and "2" (answer) which might represent "Kim" as seventy-two on the women's list. Mere mention of "man" or "lady" would, of course, cue the medium to which list was being used.

With due deference to my old friend Harry Houdini, I am not surprised that he and Bessie gave up their mind reading act, for their code needed considerable improvement, even back in the Gay Nineties, when they were working their mind reading act in dime museums. Instead of code words like "pray," new cues, such as "give," "kindly," "go on," "hurry" have been introduced. Sometimes alternates are used and a word like "next" is used for a repeat number. Thus "Tell us the next object" would be the same as using "tell" twice to represent fifty-five.

In speeding up the modern code-act, such terms as "hurry," "quickly," "go on" are very natural, and so are expressions like "good," "correct," and "right" after the medium has successfully named an object. But those words serve as cues for the next object coming up. Thus the audience man, having cued the number for "watch" is handing the watch back to its owner and reaching for a pencil with his other hand, when the medium announces, "That's a watch!" and the man promptly adds, "Right. Now what's this?" which gives the number for "pencil."

The regular code is used to represent the letters of the alphabet in numerical order, "1" for "A," "2" for "B," and so on up to "10"— which is the same as "0"— for "J." Instead of using two figures from then on, as "1-1" for "11," meaning "K" or "1-2" for "12," meaning "L," many teams use additional code words for remaining letters of the alphabet, making twenty-six in all, through to the letter "Z." Such words as "but," "also," "well, " "try," "sure," and other natural expressions serve for the additional letters.

One neat twist is to stop with "13" for the letter "K," so that only thirteen code words are needed; then begin a second set with "1" for "N," "2" for "O," "3" for "P," and so on through to "26" for "Z," using the word "next" to identify the letters as belonging to the second set. Assuming that a name like "Hugo" is not on the regular list, it could be "spelled out" with the old Houdini list, as follows: "Quickly . . . The next name, quickly . . . Speak up . . . We want the next answer." (Quickly = 8 = H. Next quickly = 21 = U. Speak = 7 = G. Next answer = 15 = O.)

This covers the groundwork of the system; and far from being crude or obvious, as it may seem in print, it is smooth and indetectable. The audience man never stresses the key words. In fact, he may often slur over them, so that they are scarcely noticed by the average listener. But the medium is trained to pick them up and is on the alert for them.

In fact, some of the techniques are quite remarkable. The Zancigs, who billed themselves as "Two Minds With But a Single

Thought," performed very deliberately and convincingly. In one test, Julius Zancig, the "professor," would have someone draw any picture or diagram on a slate, which could be shown to the audience, with the back of the slate turned toward the platform where Madame Zancig was. She wasn't blindfolded, but not only was the back of the slate turned toward her, her back was turned toward the audience, so she could work at a large blackboard set up at the rear of the platform.

Someone might draw a picture of a house, with a door, windows, and even a chimney with smoke coming out. Casually, Zancig would tell his wife to concentrate, or to go on if she hesitated. To the amazement of the audience, she would reproduce the picture on the black-board, with doors and windows of the house placed exactly and the curl of smoke issuing from the chimney as a final touch. The slow, painstaking process not only kept the audience in suspense, but enabled the professor to space his statements so they seemed much fewer than they were. Later, many obervers would swear that he scarcely talked at all.

What was more, Zancig was constantly changing his code, so he and his wife could switch back to an old one, or go into a new one, at a mere snap of the professor's fingers as a cue.

He let skeptics make phonograph recordings of
his entire act, and they were unable to trace a
code word-pattern, even though they put some
real professors of ancient languages on the job.
What really floored them was one series of tests
where Zancig used the identical words over and
over, each statement practically the same. They
brought in Chinese scholars to solve that one,
thinking that it was due to inflections of his
voice. But the Chinese scholars gave up, too.

Would you like to know why? Let Julius
Zancig tell you in his own words, as he told me.

"They were so worried about what I might
say, that they did not worry any more about the
blindfold. I mean by that, they would show me
a name on a slip of paper that my wife could not
possibly see, because she was maybe twenty,
thirty feet away. So I would give them back the
slip, and I would say to her, 'Please, just tell us
the name that I have in mind,' and soon, she
would tell it. Maybe she would ask, would I
look at it again, and I would. But always, I
would say the same thing in those same words."

So I asked, "And did she get it?"

"She always did," he replied without a smile.
"We were using our silent code."

That explained it. With a silent code, you
flash the figures one to nine by dividing your
body into nine sections, as right shoulder for

one; chest for two; left shoulder for three; then across the center of the body for four, five, six; finally at hip level, right for seven; center for eight; and left hip for nine. Simply raising a hand to your chin signifies the numeral zero. So it works just like the spoken code, but with gestures instead of words, and it is just as natural. The medium simply watches her partner's hands as he moves among the audience, asking people to whisper their names or questions or show him dollar bills, so that he can transmit the serial numbers telepathically.

But the big point was this—until Julius Zancig told me so, personally and confidentially, I never even suspected that he used a silent code. Why not? Because he talked while he used it; and that was the perfect "throw-off." While they're looking that way, you do it this way.

In contrast, there was an act called the Svengalis, which overplayed the silent code to the point where it became painful. A man worked the audience, asking for names of people, places, and things, letting the questioner raise his hand while a woman on stage gave the answer. The woman was blindfolded, so she couldn't even see the questioners when they acknowledged that she was right, which they did about ninety-nine per cent of the time.

Originally, there were two performers on the

stage, a man seated at a table and the woman at a piano, both with their backs toward the audience. If a spectator gave a famous name like "Lincoln," the man would get busy at the table and swing around toward the audience, wearing a facial makeup of Abraham Lincoln, beard and all. If a spectator called for a song like "Tea for Two," the woman on the stage immediately played it. This combination of quick-change artistry and musical talent added greatly to the entertainment value of the act. But the whole thing was too pat, too routined, to seem real. So skeptics began looking for gimmicks and soon spotted them.

First, the audience man was too conspicuous, with all his gesticulations and gyrations. The act was geared to a fast-moving tempo that made it look like the vaudeville attraction that it was, instead of the scientific demonstration that it purported to be. Since signals were being wig-wagged to somebody by the audience man, and neither of the two "mediums" on the stage could see him, skeptics rationalized that there had to be a fourth party in the act. That directed suspicion to a large, ornamental screen standing toward the rear of the stage, just beyond the two seated there.

The extra man was hidden behind the screen, peering through a narrow slit that looked like part of the design; and he was the only one who had to be familiar with the silent code. What was more, being out of sight, he could have lists fixed to the screen for rapid reference. He spotted the signals from the audience man and even had a pair of opera glasses handy for long-range operation. He then cued the "mediums" in a low tone, through the screen. The act had a good run while it lasted. Then later, it was simplified to the form first described, with a man working the audience and a woman seated on the stage, wearing a blindfold.

The man was billed as "Svengali" and the woman as "Miss Trilby," which gave the act a new slant, as Svengali was the master hypnotist of the famous novel *Trilby*, who had a girl by that name under his psychic control. In playing the part of Svengali, the audience man kept tapping his forehead or temple and making magnetic passes in Trilby's direction to keep her in a hypnotic state which enabled him to transmit the mental messages more effectively.

Actually, it gave him a "code within a code," for he divided his head into sections from one to nine, just like his body, with the chin stroke serving for zero in both cases. So by alternating hypnotic passes with body taps, each became more natural. Also, the head taps were a help to the accomplice hidden behind the screen, because he could spot them more easily than the body signals when Svengali was a long way up an aisle and somewhat obscured by the intervening audience.

I have cited the Zancigs and Svengalis in detail to illustrate the wide range between the slow, deliberate style of presentation and the fast, high-pressure type. Both did well enough in their time, but the act that topped them all, both artistically and commercially, was presented by a man named Mercedes and his partner, Madame Stanone. They played vaudeville with their act for years, and when there was no more vaudeville, they appeared in movie houses, where all that Madame Stanone needed was a piano while Mercedes worked the audience.

They specialized in one form of transmission only: musical numbers. Mercedes told members of the audience to concentrate on any selections they wanted and to ask Madame Stanone what tunes they had in mind, whereupon she would strike a few bars or an entire chorus of the desired music, which was recognized and acknowledged. It was far better than the musical portion of the old Svengali act, because Mercedes insisted that people think of the tune mentally, so that madame could pick it up directly and telepathically. At no time did Mercedes speak to Madame Stanone. He made no suspicious motions. Her back was turned to him, and there was no screen available as a hiding place for a lookout.

To top it, Mercedes gave simple instructions to each person, always in brief statements so similar that they couldn't possibly have carried a cue. Yet they did, and that was the beauty of the act. After hearing the spectator's whispered choice, Mercedes would say, "Ask for your selection," which stood for "A" in an alphabetical list of songs; or "Ask her for your selection," meaning "B" on the list; or "Ask madame for your selection" for "C"; or "Ask madame to play your selection," for "D"; or "Say, play my selection," for "E."

By prefacing those same five statements with "please," the letters F, G, H, I, J were dispatched. By using "now" as the introductory word, K, L, M, N, O were specified. By saying "will you," to start, P, Q, R, S, T were covered. By making it "won't you," the list was completed with U, V, W, X, Y, or in some cases Z.

Thus, as samples, "Please ask her for your selection" would be "G" or "Good Night Ladies" on the list; "Now, ask madame for your selection," would be "M" or "Maryland, My Maryland" on the list; "Won't you say, play my selection" would be "Y" for "Yellow Rose of Texas."

Here, the word "selection" is the key for the entire list from A through Y. For a second list, the word "music" is used instead of "selection"; for others, the words "tune," "piece," "number," "song," "melody," or simply "it" serve as keys. These lists can be doubled by stating, "Ask for the selection you want" instead of "Ask for your selection"; and so on. The act, in that form, was actually unfathomable and was a standout for many years. How it would hold up today is another question, considering the vast array of modern songs that are in frequent use.

That brings up another question, one which some people "in the know" occasionally ask me personally. They say, "Dunninger, did you ever do a code act?" and usually, they expect me to say, "No, of course not." Instead, I tell them, "Yes, naturally, because I've performed every type of mystery act there is, in order to find out which is best. And I've always settled on my own." To that, I sometimes add, "If a code act was good enough for Houdini, it was good enough for me—and that goes for handcuffs and jail escapes, too."

Actually, I specialized in escapes for a while, until I found that mentalism was more popular. I also felt that if Houdini had his field, I should have mine. That is why we won each other's esteem to the point that I became the only performer on record to fill an engagement scheduled for Houdini, when he was unable to appear; and an important engagement, too.

It was held by the Philadelphia Forum, in the Academy of Music, the city's largest auditorium. Houdini was out investigating mediums for the *Scientific American* and had to cancel a lecture date, so they called upon me instead. I put on a full evening's performance of magic and mentalism. As a novelty, I introduced a feature termed "Tri-Psycho-Mentalo," an updated version of the Svengali act in which a quick-change artist impersonated famous people selected by members of the audience. It was well received, but faded into insignificance when I presented my own "one-man" act in which I answered questions proposed to me directly.

So I followed my own trend from then on, and wisely, as events were to prove. When I put on my first radio test, some twenty years later, the head of the volunteer committee that certified the program was none other than the director of the Philadelphia Forum, who remembered the impact that my act had created in the past and was present to help launch it into what proved to be an even-greater future.

THREE

A notable pioneer in the field of mentalism was Stuart Cumberland, who billed himself as a "thought-reader," which was a very apt title. I say "apt" because there is a distinct difference between mind reading and thought-reading, as has been proven through the succeeding years. In short, you don't have to be a mind reader to be a thought-reader. Where mind reading, in the full meaning of the term, is a doubtful quantity, thought-reading not only is a proven fact, but a common occurrence. To clarify this, let us consider its various degrees from the more complex to the extremely simple.

First, we must envision a mental world akin to the physical, with the two so interlocked that certain thoughts or subconscious impressions can be studied, analyzed, and identified, just as you might test a substance in a laboratory, examine a piece of goods across a counter, or eye an object on a shelf, or at a distance. To

DUNNINGER'S SECRETS

probe the inner reaches of another person's mind, with no clue whatever as a starter and come back with a detailed account of what was going on there, would be sheer mind reading, but unfortunately, it would be practically impossible.

To pick up an overall picture, such as a scene from the past or a faraway land, would mean living it or viewing it as through another person's eyes. This in turn would mean capturing that person's mental reactions in their entirety, and therefore could be properly classed as mind reading. But technically, parapsychologists might term it *clairvoyance,* or the ability to perceive some distant or hidden thing. That is, it might be due to some function of your own inner consciousness, without the intermediary of another mind.

Personally, I do not go along with this theory. Almost every time I have had what seemed to be a pure clairvoyant experience, I have traced it to a contributing factor known as telesthesia. This important mental phenomenon has been greatly overlooked, hence it is deserving of close study, as you may find that it links with some singular experience of your own. I say this with confidence, because of my own experiences, which have been quite frequent.

In early experiments in clairvoyance, many

59

years ago, it was found that a person roused from a state of deep concentration or semitrance experienced a sensation resembling a sharp pang or a sudden shock. Even though imaginary, this could induce the equivalent of a clairvoyant vision. Such is telesthesia.

In mechanical terms, this can be likened to modern television, which in those days would have been regarded as much more remarkable than clairvoyance, as well as being much farther beyond the realm of possibility. A scanning process inaugurated by one mind induces the reconstruction of an image by another mind to which it is attuned. The clarity of the reproduction depends on the degree of attunement. But that was not all, there was a factor in telesthesia that was not recognized until television came along to explain it. Namely, the scope of the image depends upon the mind that projects it, just as the TV camera is solely responsible for what appears upon the screen. What the camera misses, the viewer misses. However, a graphic close-up, a "spot shot," so to speak, can rouse the observer's imagination to the point where he visualizes much that he did not see. Or it may be the other way about. His power of visualization may cause him to imagine that he saw more than he did.

What's more, he's very apt to be correct in his

descriptions, because he is working from the stimulus provided for that purpose. The "mental jolt" might be like glimpsing an isolated mountain peak, or being awakened by a vivid lightning flash. In the latter case, you are apt to lie there waiting for the rumble of thunder that you know should follow. If you don't hear it, you either know that the flash was more distant than you supposed; or perhaps it was something other than a lightning flash.

That's how telesthesia works. You pick up a vivid impression from another mind and others follow or suggest themselves. But it isn't mind reading; it is thought-reading. When a series of such thought impressions comes in fairly close succession, it takes on the semblance of mind reading, though if you check back, you may find that you have added links of your own making, just as you might piece together the fragments of a dream to form a waking continuity.

Telesthesia may be loosely defined as "hypnotic clairvoyance," which dates back to the time of Mesmer, who found that hypnotized subjects could diagnose ailments of other persons and even prescribe cures. Since then, there has been a succession of persons gifted with such ability—call it insight, intuition, psychic sympathy or sensitivity, whichever you prefer— the most notable modern example being Edgar

Cayce, the famous seer and metaphysical healer of Virginia Beach. The point to emphasize here is that with telesthesia, the thought-reader probes the subconscious mind of another person and picks up latent facts or impressions which that person may have forgotten, or of which he may be entirely unaware. No conscious effort is needed on the part of the person whose thoughts are being read.

The next step from the mental toward the physical is telepathy, which supplanted such terms as thought transference and mental telegraphy. Even after the word "telepathy" was coined, people continued to speak of "mental telegraphy," because it implied a conscious action on the part of the sender, with another person acting as a receiver. Years later, it was revived as "mental radio," which was even more appropriate, as it conveys the idea of one mind broadcasting at large, hoping to be picked up at random, rather than by a lone receiver.

All that is covered by telepathy, which obviously can involve physical effort both in sending and receiving, even though the transmission is a mental process. In fact, the physical phase has been so well demonstrated, that many people erroneously use the term "mental telepathy," as if it were something special. Boiled down, it comes to this: In true telepathic tests, there is a conscious effort on the part of the sender to create a mental image of an actual object, a picture, a diagram, or even written words or numbers, so that they in turn can be visualized by the receiver, just as if he saw them or heard them described aloud. But the actual transmission, instead of depending on the physical or conscious factors of sight or sound, is accomplished through their mental equivalents, as found in the subconscious.

This is by no means fanciful. Shut your eyes and you will find that you can easily recall certain scenes: a luncheon with an old friend; the hit song of a popular musical; an exciting sports event; or whatever else may spring to mind. Your recollections will include things you actually saw and heard. In addition, other sensory impressions may spring to mind, such as the grip of a handshake, the taste of a choice food, the fragrance of an exotic perfume, all belonging to the realm of reality although they are now in the past.

Shut your eyes again and picture something that you recently dreamed. If you don't dream at all, visualize what you would like to dream about, such as winning a million dollar lottery or punching somebody twice your size in the nose. Even though you know that it never happened, you can treat it as if it had, sometimes even more graphically than something that did occur.

In today's mixed-up world, many people give highly fictionized accounts of what they claim and sometimes believe are true experiences; while others disguise real life stories under the shadowy cloak of an alleged dream. All I know is that if a person concentrates strongly enough upon something that could have happened, the impression can be picked up telepathically. I say this with both assurance and sincerity, because I have often gained impressions that could not be explained in any other way. Yet if I could find a simpler explanation, I would willingly accept it.

That was what bugged them at Duke University when they initiated a very sincere effort to discover what might happen when one mind could influence another. They were loaded with assurance, too, thinking that the Zener cards, depicting arbitrary symbols, could be used as targets for telepathic tests. They invited so-called psychics of all descriptions to come down and show their wares, so naturally I was asked to come there. Just as naturally, I declined, rather than be identified with the residue of crackpots and publicity seekers who put in an appearance there.

I say "residue" with emphasis, because no-

64

body—and I mean nobody!—who had real tele-pathic ability would have reduced themselves to the kindergarten stage of experimentation that was then underway at Duke. They had the mistaken notion that you could give a person five cards, bearing the symbols circle, plus, wavy lines, square, star, and expect him to identify whichever one you decided to transmit.

My point is this: If you are forced to concen-trate on symbols of that sort, you will complete-ly ruin your telepathic talent, if you have any. In order to choose one, you must reject the others, and if you hesitate too long on one, the receiver may pick it as your choice, thereby eliminating the symbol that you actually have in mind.

What may have misled Zener in the first place was the fact that early telepathic tests had been highly successful with playing cards, so he assumed that geometric figures would be easier. But he overlooked the more important fact that playing cards were already familiar objects to many people; and with children, in particular, tests with playing cards were like trying a new game.

I had known this for years before Duke University began its tests and in all my demon-strations, I used playing cards, emphasizing that I wanted bridge addicts and poker players to visualize cards so I could pick up impressions of them. Some of the spontaneous results were fabulous, because playing cards, with persons who know and like them, are a language in themselves. John O'Neill, then science editor of the *Brooklyn Daily Eagle*, devoted columns to my tests with playing cards, but when I offered to do tests for Duke experimenters, under conditions endorsed by John O'Neill, they froze. Nothing would count unless done in their parapsychological laboratory with their five-symbol cards, with which they would gladly test me.

So the people who were not getting results wanted the man who was getting them to switch from the proven to the doubtful. Naturally, I didn't, which shows that I am perhaps as prophetic as I am telepathic, for while the Duke tests were still getting more criticism than recognition, I went on the air over a national network and became the radio sensation of that year and years to follow, presenting the very type of convincing demonstrations that I had been doing all along.

Understand, I am not one of the critics of the Duke tests. On the contrary, I feel that they did more to further all types of mentalism than anything else could have. The cautious, painstaking methods adopted by Dr. Rhine and his associates created considerable interest and confidence in their experiments in extrasensory perception, or ESP, as they termed clairvoyance, telesthesia, telepathy, and other mental by-products such as precognition or prophecy, by rolling them all into one big ball of wax.

Eventually, they agreed that colors might be better suited to ESP tests than geometric symbols. Also, it should be noted that some of the most phenomenal runs of correct hits were scored by Duke students rather than by outsiders. Both those factors go along with my claim that familiarity with the objects used—as in the case of playing cards—is essential toward good results. But the big reason for running tests with their own cards, on their own grounds, under their own conditions was to make sure that no trickery was involved. An odd touch, because according to some critics, the Duke ESP lab was a setup for fakery at a time when some remarkable scores were made.

That brings us to the next phase of thought-reading, where physical factors begin to supplant the mental. Here, the vital link is *hyperesthesia,* which can be defined as an intensification of ordinary senses to the point where they can pick up impressions that they would not normally receive. Thus in contrast to extrasensory perception, it might be classed as supersensory. Almost everyone has experienced hyperesthesia to some degree; and numerous examples could be cited in ordinary life.

Take the proofreader, who can spot misspelled words by simply glancing at a printed page; the bird watcher, who can catch a distant call; the jeweler who places gems in a setting; the wine taster, who can name the year of a vintage; the nonsmoker who can smell a cigarette before someone lights it. It should be noted that in such cases, one sense is favored at the expense of others; and usually, the person involved realizes that he has focused his attention on the question of immediate importance, to the exclusion of all else.

That is simply the steppingstone to hyperesthesia, in which the subject does not know that he has sensed something beyond normalcy. He is so concentrated upon his purpose that he excludes everything else. In short, he is in an autohypnotic condition, so he does not recall any secondary or irrelevant impressions that may have contributed to his main objective. This, I have long known from my own experiments with hypnotized subjects, whom I have placed in the very mood that I have just described. But getting back to experiments in ESP before the term was even coined, keen scientists attributed the success of certain telepathic tests to hyperesthesia, for this reason:

They noted that when a sender was concentrating on an object, his mental effort produced a physical result in the form of involuntary whispering. The motion of the sender's lips were plainly visible to the observers, but not to the receiver, who was either blindfolded or facing the other way. Yet the receiver caught the sender's message. So to double-check the process, one observer stayed close to the sender; another observer stationed himself beside the receiver. Observer A saw the sender's lips move; Observer B heard nothing. Yet the thought projected by the sender was repeated word for word by the receiver!

So the experimenters rigged a huge, concave shell, some eight feet in diameter, and placed it behind the receiver, while the sender concentrated on an object. Sure enough, the big shell acted like an echo chamber. Experimenters who stayed close to it could catch the faint but audible whisper that the sender was projecting to the receiver, on an involuntary basis. But that still left the question: Take away the metal shell and how could the whisper be heard at all? The answer was, through hyperesthesia. The receiver was so keyed up that he could hear what other listeners couldn't—that is, without the help of the shell—just as the sender was willing to swear that he hadn't whispered anything, even though observers had seen him do exactly that.

I discussed this phenomenon with a scientific editor, who still had doubts regarding it. He felt that telesthesia was still a better answer than hyperesthesia, favoring the mental over the physical for a very good reason. He and his wife were tuned to the same mental beam in an amazing way. He commuted to New York from Scarsdale and always went back on the same train, which she would meet with the car, unless he phoned her, saying that he would be coming on an earlier train. But occasionally, when that happened, he didn't have time to put the call through, so he would decide to call the house after he reached Scarsdale.

But he never had to do that. Always, whether by human hunch, woman's intuition, or better still, sheer telepathy, his wife had caught the message and was there at the station, waiting for him. When I commented that maybe she had been there a few times when he hadn't shown up on an earlier train, he vehemently insisted that it had never happened that way. To prove it, he would have his wife confirm the statement. She happened to be coming into New York for lunch that very day, so he suggested that I go with him to Grand Central Station and meet her when she came from the train.

I agreed and we went there. While we were waiting at the gate on the lower level, where the local trains came in, the editor jokingly suggested that perhaps he could read his wife's mind better than I could. So I countered that by handing him a small pad and a pencil, saying that I wanted him to write the first word that came to his mind, then fold the slip and put it in his pocket. He did that and I told him, "Now we'll see who can really read your wife's mind, you or I. But don't mention any details until I say so."

He agreed. When his wife came from the train, he introduced us, and I told her, "I want to try a telepathic test. But it's noisy here with so many people coming from the train. Let's go where it's quieter." So we went up steps from the lower level to the wide, inclined corridors that lead upward. There we were in a domed enclosure, some thirty feet square, with nobody else around, so I said, "This will do."

I said to the lady, "You stand in this corner, while I go over there to the far corner. When I am there, I want you to just whisper a word to your husband. I'll write the word that occurs to me on this pad, and we'll see how it works out. Agreed?"

She agreed, and we did exactly that. I was some thirty feet away when I wrote a word on the pad, folded the slip, came back, and handed it to her husband. In those days, men wore vests, and I remember how meticulously he put my slip in one vest pocket, but kept his own in the opposite pocket. Then we went to lunch and after soup was served, the editor became itchy and said to me, "I guessed wrong, Dunninger, but I want to see how close you came to guessing right. So how about showing my wife the slips?"

I replied, "Of course, but first, what was the word?"

"Bolero."

"And how close did you come?"

"Not very close," he admitted, opening his slip. "I wrote the word 'Market,' as you can see."

"A wide guess," I agreed. "Now hand your wife the slip I gave you and let her read it for herself."

He did just that, and his wife went so goggle-eyed that he snatched the slip from her and read it for himself. There it was, a single word that scored a one hundred per cent hit: *Bolero.*

If any two people were ever sold on telepathy, they were, right then. But since I had presented the test to prove another point, I promptly disillusioned them. I reminded the editor that he and I had discussed the subject of hyperesthesia and how whispers could be picked up by a concave sound reflector; but he wouldn't go along with me.

"That couldn't apply in this case," he insisted. "You're just trying to cover up for a genuine telepathic test, because you don't want to run the risk of trying to repeat it. Picking up a whisper would have been impossible, because you were out in the open, over forty feet away, and my wife's whisper was so low that even I could scarcely hear her. What was more, you'd placed her so her back was to you, and your back was turned, too, so you couldn't possibly have read her lips. You unquestionably read her thought; and if it wasn't telepathy, what was it?"

I told him that I had already told him. When he still was nonplussed, I spelled it out in detail. When he and his wife learned how neatly I had baffled them, they were as impressed as if I had performed a feat of bona fide telepathy. My secret was simply this: I happened to know that the domed landing, just up the short steps from the lower level at Grand Central, was a miniature whispering gallery, an architectural curiosity usually found on a larger scale. I had tried it a few times, but had never intended to put it to special use, until this chance opportunity had occurred.

DUNNINGER'S SECRETS

I had purposely picked the square landing for the thought-reading test and had placed the editor's wife so that she faced one corner of the wall. I took my stance in the opposite corner, facing the other way, not just to prove that I could not see her lips move, but for the far more important reason that it was the only way in which I could catch even her slightest whisper. The distance of forty feet meant nothing; actually, her whisper carried considerably farther, for it traveled up the corner of the wall, along the curved ceiling, and down into my corner, where I heard the word "Bolero" as distinctly as her husband did, over in her corner.

We went back to Grand Central later, so I could show them exactly how it worked. If you want to try it yourself, you can, because the place is still there, right where the ramps descending from the upper level meet; and there is seldom anybody there. You can tell your friends that you are telepathic and prove it to their satisfaction; or you can play it straight and just have fun whispering back and forth. But you'd better hurry, for they've torn down Penn Station, and Grand Central may be next.

I have given this in detail for several reasons: First, it shows the importance of actually demonstrating anything that depends on subterfuge instead of merely explaining it. Unless people are baffled to begin with, the real impact is missed, and they are apt to shrug it off as something that couldn't fool them—though they are always likely to be fooled by something even simpler, later. Second, this shows how a seemingly unimportant or airtight detail can be overlooked, thereby deepening the mystery. In suggesting that the editor's wife whisper the word to him for corroboration, I stressed as absolute precautions the very factors that were making the result possible.

There was also an offshoot, which makes this case a standout, because it leads right into the next phase of thought-reading that involves physical factors and therefore plays a more important role than people usually suppose; namely, *thought coincidence.*

After thinking it over, the editor said, "Well, Dunninger, you've proven the need for caution where telepathic tests are concerned, but you still haven't explained how my wife knows when and where to meet me, as well as other things that have surprised us."

To that, I countered, "Tell me, just why did you write the word 'market' on your slip? Was there a special reason?"

"Come to think of it, there was," he admitted. "They've just opened a new market near our home, and when I left this morning, my wife spoke about going there."

"But I didn't have time, today," his wife

chimed in. "If I had, I guess the word 'market' would have been uppermost in my mind."

That fitted with the point I wanted to make. I had them think back to other morning incidents that might have planted ideas in their minds. The editor recalled that occasionally, when his wife was driving him to the station, he had mentioned that he would try to get away from work early and would phone her if he could. Getting no call, she could have subconsciously supposed that he had definitely said he would be coming on the early train, so she had gone to meet it. From that, they traced back to other incidents where thoughts had apparently flashed between them, with times when both had changed their minds, yet had forgotten it.

This was quite understandable to me, because it linked with hypnotism, on which I am highly conversant. One important phase is autohypnosis, in which a person is so absorbed by his inward thoughts that he becomes unaware of other things; "daydreaming," as it is sometimes called. If a hypnotist finds a subject who will go into such a state practically of his own accord, all the hypnotist has to do is play along with it, much like a ventriloquist talking without moving his lips and letting the dummy take the credit. When two people who are well acquainted become absorbed in their own thoughts, both

76

may fall into a mildly autohypnotic state and plan or discuss something, without realizing that they have come to some agreement.

This might be termed "mutual hypnosis," and if you look back in your own experience, you may be surprised to find how often it may have worked in your case. Often, it is coupled with the phase known as posthypnosis, in which an impression submerged in the subconscious mind suddenly comes to the fore, as though it were a new idea or a sudden inspiration. That's when it takes on the semblance of a telepathic flash when two people are involved.

However, that does not rule out telepathy or other forms of ESP. On the contrary, mutual hypnosis induces the very conditions regarded as ideal for such phenomena. In early telepathic experiments, it was found that hypnotized subjects scored higher than when in the normal state. So it is difficult to tell where telepathy leaves off and thought coincidence takes over. My own opinion, based upon long experience, is that one merges into the other. In the great majority of the thousands of performances that I have given, I have often struck upon coinciding thoughts with total strangers, quick flashes that seem to come from nowhere, yet prove to be right. But they have been far too frequent to be charged off to chance alone, particularly when one "hit" leads to another and sometimes several more.

This brings us to another blend of the mental with the physical, or you might say the psychic and the psychological; namely, *linked thoughts.* Where a thought coincidence depends upon an outside stimulus that produces a fixed result, linked thoughts provide their own developments, as a simple comparison will show.

Consider a small community living near a large gasoline refinery. An explosion is suddenly heard, followed by a rattling of windows. It might be an airplane breaking the sound barrier, or a blast from a distant quarry, or a truck backfiring somewhere on the block. But to everybody hearing it, one thought will jump to mind: "The refinery!" That would be *thought coincidence,* but in such a case it would be obvious that people would think alike.

Put that same explosion in a quiet, rural community with no gasoline refinery, and wild guesses would result, ranging from the breaking of the sound barrier, a quarry blast, boys playing with firecrackers, an earthquake, or a surprise bombing raid. Each would start a chain reaction in different minds; and if two sets of *linked thoughts* should cross, as they sometimes do, it would seem more than mere coincidence. A good example would be two persons rushing to the local hospital, each thinking the other had been taken there as a victim of the mystery blast, only to meet at the door and find that they were both uninjured.

Again, telepathy could be a factor, as it often is in time of stress, but crossed chains of linked thoughts may also be the result of stylized *thought patterns.* These play a remarkable part in everyday life and can be used to great advantage in tracing the inner workings of a person's mind. Once you peg a person's thought pattern, you can tell him what he is going to think before he thinks it, and you keep one or more steps ahead, sometimes playing hunches to a point where your ability seems uncanny, even to yourself.

To reduce thought patterns to basic terms, let me recite my experience with an editor for whom I was preparing material on fraudulent spirit mediums, a good many years ago. The editor was both exacting and methodical, as he had to be when dealing with factual material. He had a practical approach to everything, as the success of his magazine proved, and he felt that he could tune in on the mass mind of his readers, with which I fully agreed. He, in turn was amazed at my ability in playing hunches and wanted to know if I could apply it in his case.

79

So I did. I picked up a pad, removed a sheet of paper and tore it into four slips. I wrote something on each, folded the sheets and placed them in front of him. I handed him the pad and if you want to check the test for yourself, get a pad and pencil, so you can go along with it. Or you can try it on other people, by reading my statements aloud and letting them follow them.

I said, "I want you to concentrate on some simple everyday things, so you can catch my thoughts as I project them. I'll set the pace and you make the choice. Agreed?"

He agreed, so I said, "Take a simple digit—a figure from one to five and write it on the pad. Just as it comes to your mind."

He did that and I told him, "Now, close your eyes and concentrate on a color. Just name a simple color and write it on the pad."

Again, he complied quite promptly, and I continued, "Now, an article of furniture. Visualize it and write it down next."

He went through that process so promptly that I tacked on another option, "Just think of a flower. Add its name to the list."

That done, I told him to open the slips in order and compare my projection with his reception. He did. With each slip that he read, his forehead furrowed more deeply and at the finish, he asked in an awed tone, "You mean our minds work that simply? Like pressing buttons, so we have no minds of our own? Is that why you called the turn on me?"

"You called the turn yourself," I replied. "When you told me how you tuned in on the mass mind, I knew you would have to follow thought patterns. So I gave you an individual test of the thought pattern type, and you responded as I expected. That proves that we were both right."

Here is what I wrote on my four slips:
The figure —— 3
The color —— RED
Furniture —— CHAIR
The flower —— ROSE
Here is what the editor wrote on his pad:
3 — RED — CHAIR — ROSE

When these choices are analyzed, it becomes obvious that they should naturally spring to mind. The figure "3" represents the midpoint, or balance, between one and five. Red is the first color of the spectrum, or rainbow, and the first used in naming the colors of the American flag. A chair is the commonest article of furniture, and the editor was sitting on one when I handed him the pad. The rose is the predominant flower of song and story. So that should clinch it all along the line— or should it? Let's see.

When we left the office, the editor couldn't

wait to try the test on a writer who was meeting us for lunch. I suggested that he work it himself.

When the editor remarked that he had been developing telepathic powers, the writer gave me a somewhat skeptical glance; then decided to see what the editor had to show. So the editor went ahead with it, just as I had shown him, in methodical, letter-perfect style. But when the writer opened the editor's slips and compared them with what he had written on the pad, he was not astonished in the least. Instead, he simply smiled.

The editor's slips read: 3—RED—CHAIR —ROSE.

The writer's pad stated: 4—BLUE—TABLE —ORCHID.

While the test was under way, I had written out a slip of my own, folded it and placed it beneath a plate. Now, I told the writer to lift the plate, unfold my slip and read it. This time he really was surprised.

On my slip I had written: 4—BLUE—TABLE.

Again I had called the turn where the thought pattern was concerned: and again the analysis is obvious. Where the editor wanted to prove something to his own satisfaction and had therefore stayed with each original choice, the writer, who wanted to disprove it, had automatically dismissed or rejected the first thought that

came to his mind and had swung to the next, not
realizing that he was forming a secondary pattern quite as stylized as the first.

Rejecting "3," he had gone one number higher, naming "4." The color "red" when it came to
mind had immediately made him think of "red,
white and blue," so he had rejected "red" and
taken "blue." Also, rejection of "chair" led to
his acceptance of "table" as the next most
common article of furniture. The editor had
unwittingly clinched it; for instead of handing
the pad to the writer, he laid it on the table in
front of him, making "table" a natural choice.

I could see all that coming up the moment the
writer flashed his skeptical glance my way.
You've heard of "second guessers." I labeled
him a "second chooser," an easy type to spot,
once you get used to them. True to form, he
tried to cover up his puzzlement by raising a
criticism.

"I notice," he said, "that you left the flower
out. How come you couldn't guess that I had
'orchid' in mind?"

"Because I don't guess at such things," I
replied. "Unless I pick up a clear impression, I
drop it. In this case, the fault was yours. You
were thinking of different flowers and when
'orchid' popped to your mind, you wrote it
down; but by then you were thinking of some

other flower, so orchid wasn't a real choice."

I was applying sound logic, because once "rose" is rejected, almost any flower might be chosen. The writer didn't realize this, but he nodded that I was right.

"A funny thing," he said. "I was thinking of roses to start; first one kind, then another. But I shied away from them very fast and began picturing other flowers; and when 'orchid' popped up, as you say, I just decided to let it go at that."

"But you shouldn't have gone that far," I told him. "You should have stopped with 'lily'—or even better, with 'daffodil.'"

His jaw really dropped at that. He swung to the editor and exclaimed, "The man's incredible! Do you know, those were the very flowers I was going to write down—'lily' and 'daffodil'— and when I couldn't decide which, I took 'orchid' on the offbeat." He turned to me and fairly blurted, "How did you know all that?"

"Through telepathy," put in the editor, and when the writer agreed, "Yes, that must be it," I let it go at that. I didn't tell the writer that he had given me the cue himself. When he said that he had thought of different kinds of roses, I knew that he had colors in mind: red, white, yellow. That meant that he would think of other flowers in terms of those colors, which made "lily white" a sure shot and a "yellow daffodil" a good follow-up. Here, I was letting him set the thought pattern and I was simply following it, which proves my point all the more.

Of course, you must watch out for snags in such tests. You may encounter a maverick who will write "1½" for a number, "puce" for a color, "Quaker lady" for a flower, and "cuspidor" for an article of furniture. If the writer had been one of those jokers, I would simply have left my slip under the plate without mentioning it at all. Personally, I screen such characters beforehand, by learning something of their likes and dislikes, or sounding them out by working a test with a more susceptible person and watching their reactions.

Another way is to proceed step by step. In that case, you tell a person to think of a number between one and ten, which apparently allows a lot of leeway, but the chances are very strong that he will pick "7." You don't need a slip in this case, you just say, "I get the impression of '7'—right?" If he says, "Yes," that's fine; if he says, "No," you say, "Wait—keep concentrating —it's an odd number—" If he says, "Yes," you tell him, "3."

If you hit with "7," he's a pretty sure bet for "red," "chair," and "rose." With "3," he may waver to "blue" or "table," so you will have to use your own judgment with those; and then decide whether to use a flower as a follow-up. But if he picked an even number between one and ten, you can tell him you were simply testing him for "positive" or "negative" impressions, and then switch to something else. That is, unless you become so skilled at the game that you can follow your own hunches, as I do.

I once tested an English professor and kept telling him his impressions were so negative that it was very difficult to read his thoughts, until I had him think of a flower. Then, to his amazement, I hit "chrysanthemum" right on the nose. Afterward, he complimented me on really having picked up a negative impression, because he hadn't been concentrating on actual flowers; he had been thinking of their names and when he came to "chrysanthemum," he decided that it was so hard to spell, he would surely stump me with it.

Maybe it was telepathic, or perhaps, since I knew he was an English professor, and would think in terms of words, I followed the natural thought pattern and formed a chain of linked thoughts that resulted in a perfect thought coincidence. I remembered that case so vividly that when I was trying the same test with a German professor, who also adopted a skeptical attitude, I played another hunch when he was concentrating on a flower and came up with "edelweiss." That was exactly what he had in mind. He was not the only one dumfounded when he read it on the slip that I had handed him—I was even more so. Actually, I couldn't remember ever hearing the word "edelweiss" until that hunch hit me. But later, thinking back, I vaguely recalled it from years before, but I had always thought that it was a beer, not a flower.

Note that an initial suggestion—as "number," "color," "furniture," "flower," is needed to establish a thought pattern with a resultant thought coincidence. Sometimes the suggestion can be stepped up to a degree where the coincidence is automatic, either by a sensory stimulus or a memory jog. First, let me give a classic example that I introduced years ago, which is still as good as ever, if worked with someone of the proper suggestibility, or you might say susceptibility.

I reached in my pocket and brought out a case containing a pack of playing cards and held it upright in front of the person's eyes, as I said, "Here is a case containing a standard pack of playing cards. I want you to think of a card in that pack, a card that comes naturally to your mind. When you have fixed on it, keep it constantly in mind. You have it? Good. Name it."

My subject responded, "The ace of spades."

"Open the case," I told him. "Go through the pack and pick out your card, the ace of spades."

He opened the case, took out the pack, went through it, card by card, and looked up blankly, saying, "It isn't here."

"Naturally not," I told him, as I reached in my pocket and brought out the ace of spades, "because I removed it from the pack before you even thought of it!"

The subtle suggestion behind this test depends upon the brand of playing cards used. This may come as a surprise, since the cards were still in the case when the ace of spades was chosen, but that is where the answer lies. The proper cards are "Bicycles," because the printing on the outside of the card case includes a full-sized ace of spades—without the index corners—as part of the design. When this is held in front of the person's eyes while he is being told to "think of a card," the impression of the ace of spades is implanted in his mind. But it should be handled casually, not flaunted too obviously. Also, turn that side of the card case downward when you hand it to him, so he can open it and look for the card he named.

That is, if he named the "ace of spades." If he didn't, open the case yourself, look through the pack for his card and use it for some other test. Here, a skilled card worker's routine would be to spread the faces of the cards toward himself, cut the pack when he comes to the card named —say, the ten of hearts—and palm off the card. He would then hand the pack to the spectator, telling him to find the card himself. While that was going on, he would bring the palmed card from his pocket, saying that he'd just remembered that he had put it there beforehand, knowing it would be chosen.

Years ago, I had phenomenal results with a "time test," which I presented as follows: I took a sheet of paper about five inches square and drew a circle three inches in diameter. I then marked the circle with numbers from one to twelve, exactly like a watch dial, even decorating it with a stem-winder above the number twelve.

I gave the paper and a pencil to a man who seemed to be a suitable subject, and told him, "While my back is turned, I want you to close your eyes and visualize a watch dial. Think of it on a large scale, then picture the hands set at whatever time occurs to you. Then mark those hands exactly on the clock dial that I drew on this sheet of paper. But make sure my back is turned while you are doing it. You understand?"

He nodded that he understood, so I added, "Then fold the paper in half; and fold it in half

again. Then put it in front of you where everyone can see it. But do nothing unless my back is
turned. You understand?"

Again he nodded that he did, so I turned my
back and let him go ahead. But for the benefit of
other people who could see what I was doing, I
brought a watch from my pocket, twisted the
stem-winder, and held the watch face downward until the subject said that he had folded
the slip as required.

Then I swung around, laid the watch face up
on the table and announced, "This is the time I
had in mind. I projected it to your mind. Tell me
if it happened to be right."

My watch was set at twenty minutes after
eight: 8:20. Usually, the subject didn't reply.
Instead, he opened his slip, slowly, almost
numbly, and laid it beside my watch. The hands
that he had marked on the dial were at exactly
8:20.

This test depended on a "memory jog" and a
very neat one. Back when I first introduced it,
there were many neighborhood jewelry stores
that specialized in watch repairs, and they all
had big painted watches hanging in the window
or over the door. They were as common in those
days as a striped pole outside a barber's shop or
three balls over a pawnshop—symbols which
are still seen today. The painted hands on those

wooden dummies were always permanently set at 8:20, probably because it gave the sign a symmetrical appearance. People were so familiar with them that the average adult would automatically picture a watch dial with the hands at that position; a purely subconscious impression.

It was better than the "ace" on the card case, because the person already had the time of 8:20 in mind, but it had this drawback. With cards I could switch to any of several tests if the ace of spades didn't register; but with the watch, there was no way out. So, surefire though it generally was, I had to devise an alternate procedure.

I came up with the following: Whenever the subject saw the time was wrong, I could tell it by his expression before he could even say so. Promptly, I would say, "You didn't wait long enough to pick up the impression I projected. So we'll do it the other way around. You set the watch at the time you have in mind, and I'll draw a dial showing it. But wait until I've turned my back. Fair enough?"

Naturally it was, and the person would therefore agree. I would pick up his folded slip, saying, "We won't need this," and tear it across, then place the pieces together, and tear them across again, dropping them in my pocket. After that, I picked up a pad and pencil, turned my

91

back, and told him, "Now set the dial and lay the watch face down on the table."

Assume that he set the watch at 11:15 and had it lying face down when I finished my diagram and laid the pad face down beside it, telling him to turn both up. Imagine the gasp from the onlookers when they saw that I had drawn a big dial and marked the hands in heavily, pointing to 11:15 just like the watch. Amazing indeed, so amazing that everybody forgot the little paper slip that I had torn up and put away, yet it held the answer.

The square was first folded into quarters; then I tore it twice across, apparently making sixteen tiny pieces. But of those, the central four were still intact. I kept that center square in one hand, while I dropped the twelve other pieces into my pocket with my right hand. When I turned away, I simply opened the center square that I had retained, and there was the dial that the subject had drawn, showing the hands at 11:15. So I drew a similar dial on the pad, but much bigger, and the job was done.

Later, when the old jeweler's signs went out of style, but people still wanted me to do the "time test," I eliminated the preliminaries and simply handed a person a square sheet with a dial already drawn on it and told him to mark. the hands wherever he wanted them, then fold it across the creases and keep the time in mind, while I tore up the slip and disposed of the pieces. Of course, I kept the center square and had ample chance to open it while I was turning the hands of a watch, which I set accordingly. Then it was just a matter of laying the watch face down, so the person could name the time that he had in mind, then turn up the watch to prove that I had caught the thought.

Try it yourself, and you will be surprised how easily it works. But be sure to drop that center square in your pocket while all eyes are on the watch. Of course, there's another way of working it without the slip, one that I've used to nonplus the deep-dyed skeptics. I hand a watch to a person and tell him to set the hands while I'm out of the room and let other people see the time so they can all concentrate on it. Then he's to turn the hands to another position, say twelve o'clock, and call me back in. All I have to do is turn the hands, lay the watch face down and when they turn up the watch, it shows the time they all have in mind.

All I need for that near-miracle is a special watch and a well-lighted room. The face of the watch is coated with luminous paint, but the hands and numerals are quite ordinary. When I show the watch under a strong light, it looks ordinary, too, but the luminous paint begins absorbing the light. A person sets it, say at 2:30, and while he's showing it around, the hands block the light from the dial. He then turns the hands to 12 o'clock. When I come in, all I have to do is take the watch and turn my back to the light, so the face of the watch will glow. There, the shadows left by the hands will show the exact time at which to set them again, like ghostly guideposts. So that's where I put them!

FOUR

In one special sense, the most outstanding witness of my demonstrations of mentalism was Thomas Alva Edison, the famous inventor who was aptly styled "The Wizard of Menlo Park." Actually, Edison's wizardry was far greater than that of many so-called mediums and mystics who claimed that they could produce assorted phenomena from table tipping to the materialization of spirit forms. Yet Edison was keenly interested in such matters for the simple reason that his own ability to turn the impossible into reality had encouraged him to keep an open mind toward anything unexplainable until sufficient evidence was gathered to disprove it.

There was, of course, this distinct difference: All of Edison's endeavors had been in the physical realm, whereas those of pretended mediums were in the psychic. But he was familiar enough with the absurd claims and wild dreams of unsuccessful inventors, particularly those who went in for "perpetual motion" gadgets, to recognize the extremes to which delusions could be carried. Hence he was virtually immune to the frauds that fake mediums had perpetrated on Sir William Crookes, Sir Oliver Lodge, and other noted scientists. From Edison's practical viewpoint, the logical link between the physical and psychic might be found in mental phenomena. That was why he was so interested in my work that he paid me the compliment of saying, "Never have I witnessed anything as mystifying or as seemingly impossible."

I was more than flattered by this testimonial, because it cleared up a false claim involving Mr. Edison that had persisted for many years. Back before World War I, a clever mentalist named Bert Reese, who called himself "Doctor Reese," created a stir among European scientists by reading and answering questions that had been written on slips of paper which people folded and placed in their pockets or other places where Reese could have no access to them. Among those impressed by Reese's prowess was the noted French psychic investigator, Charles Richet, who coined the term "cryptesthesia" to cover clairvoyance and telepathy, long before anyone thought of the phrase extrasensory perception.

Richet cited such authorities as Baron Schrenck Notzing and Dr. Joseph Maxwell to prove that Reese's powers were real; and there is no question that Reese did produce some remarkable results, although they were strictly phoney. What made them wrong was this: When Reese came to America, he cited Richet and others to prove that his message reading was evidence of a still greater ability which Richet himself accepted; for Richet stated, somewhat naively, "Reese tells of many interviews with prominent men, especially with leading American financiers; for one of his gifts was the ability to discover springs of water and also oil wells."

That had all the elements of an outright con game and when Reese even puzzled Hereward Carrington, who had exposed many of the tricks of fake mediums and psychics, he was on his way toward building a clientele of grade-A suckers. To clinch it, Reese wangled a meeting with Edison and put over some of his surprising stunts.

The peak of Reese's performance was this: He asked Edison to go into another room and write a question, which Edison did. The question was, "Is there anything better than hydroxide of nickel for an alkaline electric battery?" He then returned to the room where Reese was and

DUNNINGER'S SECRETS

Reese declared, "No, there is nothing better than hydroxide of nickel for an alkaline battery." That sounded amazing enough, and when Charles Richet, in recording it, added that Reese "immediately answered" Edison's question, it approached the miraculous.

To top that, Richet also reported that two years later, Reese paid Edison a surprise visit. On that occasion, Edison wrote the word "Keno" in tiny letters on a slip of paper that he put into his pocket. When Edison asked Reese what he had written," Reese answered "Keno" without hesitation.

Oddly, Richet and other scientists and investigators couldn't read between their own lines when they eagerly recorded facts that they thought were so important while leaving out others that were even more essential. It was obvious that Reese was trying to "promote" Edison and that his "surprise" visit was strictly a "follow-up" on that score. Maybe Reese was counting on Edison as a friend in court, because along about that time, he was arrested in New York City on a "disorderly conduct" charge, which was another term for "fortune telling." He managed to beat the rap by getting the judge to write questions on three slips and put them in different pockets, whereupon Reese "read" the questions correctly in his usual smart style.

That resulted in dismissal of the charges, but it also revealed a fact that Reese didn't want publicized; namely, that he was unable to read just one slip. Reese needed a few slips to start!

I was already sure of that, for some of Richet's accounts had told how Reese had answered "many" questions, instead of only one, as if that made it all the more wonderful. But I wanted corroboration of the Edison case from the one man who I was sure could give me the exact details, Mr. Edison himself. While I was considering how I might meet him, the opportunity came my way of its own accord. Edison had heard of my work and being still interested in the possibility of a mental link between the physical and the psychic, he arranged to witness one of my demonstrations.

Understand, this was a paid engagement in which I appeared strictly as an entertainer, the only way in which I ever have or ever will accept a fee for my services. That leaves me free to present any tests in any way I want, without disclosing or discussing any of my methods or anybody else's. In this instance, however, I was anxious to talk to Mr. Edison in order to satisfy myself regarding the Bert Reese episode. It turned out that he was equally eager to talk to me about it. When he told me that he had never witnessed anything so seemingly impossible as my performance, I asked him how it compared with others and that promptly brought up the "readings" that he had obtained from Reese.

As I suspected, Bert had asked Edison to write several questions on each occasion and had answered most of them, but not immediately, as Richet had reported. Reese had "staggered" the questions and answers, so to speak, answering some before the others had been written; and his answers had all followed the same pattern, that of simply duplicating the questions, as with the mention of "hydroxide of nickel" and the word "Keno." When Edison asked me point blank to what extent I felt mind reading had been involved, I replied emphatically, "With all due respect to Doctor Reese, anyone who simply repeats anything that has been written on a folded slip is a slip reader, not a mind reader."

I have used that statement in my opening remarks in nearly all my performances ever since, for the very good reason that Mr. Edison was definitely impressed by it. What was more, he was still further impressed by a special test I gave him to illustrate that very point. I asked him to write a question on a slip of paper, as he had with Reese, emphasizing that I intended to do the test with one question only. I also specified that the question should pertain to something that he had in mind only, that it should not be mentioned directly in the question, as in both instances with Reese.

Edison nodded his agreement. He wrote the question privately, and I insisted that he hold it in his closed right hand while I pressed the fingers of my left hand against his left wrist. Taking a pencil in my right hand, I closed my eyes, concentrated and spelled out, letter by letter, the word O-S-M-I-U-M, on a pad of paper. Frankly, I wasn't familiar with the word at that time, but Mr. Edison was. He opened his folded question and handed it to me.

It read: "What metallic element do I have in mind?"

"That was it," said Edison, pointing to my slip. "Osmium."

Speaking still more frankly, after all these years, I did not have the slightest idea that osmium was a metallic element, but I do know that it was the word that Edison had in mind. What is more, when I explained to him how I had gained the answer, not just the question, he dismissed the Reese episode as trickery, which it was. I had the privilege of giving him many further demonstrations, some even more remarkable, as his quoted testimony proves. But to me, my great achievement was spiking the old Reese rumor, which still is quoted, but only by nonentities who will soon be as forgotten as Reese himself.

Except that Doctor Reese should not be forgotten, because he was a standout in his own right. The mere fact that he drew reputable scientists like Richet into such a trap—they are always falling into traps, by the way—or, in this case, into such a trap that they could almost drag down a great mind—such as Edison's— along with them, is reason enough to expose the whole phoney business. Again, this is no reflection on Doctor Reese, who certainly was not a doctor and whose name was probably not Reese. He is to be pitied, not condemned, because he was not only years ahead, but miles ahead, of some of our modern mystics who are now duping the public far beyond any extent that he ever envisioned.

But it is reason enough to reveal how he did it, as a prelude to explaining how they do it. So here is the bitter, but unvarnished truth:

Bert Reese depended upon one of the oldest and perhaps the boldest of all devices used by message-reading mediums in their phoney work, a trick that for a century or more has been known to the trade as the "one ahead." As commonly performed by itinerant fakers, it boils down to this—a batch of questions are gathered from an audience and placed in a bowl, or anything else convenient. The medium picks up one, holds it to his—or her—forehead and avows, "I have a question from a woman named Lucille. A very personal question regarding an appointment one week from Friday. Will Lucille please acknowledge this, so I can answer it?"

Nobody responds, so the medium opens the question, studies it and declares, "I am not going to read Lucille's question. It's really too personal, so I'd rather not embarrass her, if she is still here. But I rather suspect that she is the young lady that I saw go out while the questions were still being written. Now that I know what she had on her mind, I'm not at all surprised that she left."

Now, it so happens that there was no Lucille in the audience and therefore no such question. It is simply a bit of fakery, enabling the medium to pick up some legitimate question, open it and read it under the pretense that it was written by the imaginary Lucille. What the medium really reads is something such as, "Should I go through with my present investment? John G." So the medium lays that aside as if it was Lucille's and picks up another folded message. Placing it to his forehead, the medium announces confidently, "This question gives me the vibration of J.G. A man with the initials J.G.

Will he please acknowledge it?" As a man raises his hand, the medium adds, "Ah, there you are John. Your name *is* John, isn't it? What you want to know is whether your business will make out well. It should, because you have been putting money in it. Correct? Stay with it, John."

The medium opens the message now in hand, smiles and says, "That's right. Your question says, 'Should I go through with my investment' —and you have heard my answer." What the medium is actually reading is another question, asking, "Does Bob really love me? Marie." So the medium is again working one ahead; and keeps on—and on—with the same game until time runs out.

Sometimes a medium has a stooge play the part of "Lucille." Like the other customers, she drops a question into the bowl, but gives it an extra fold, so the medium can tell it from the rest. The medium picks any random question, treats it as "Lucille's," but in this case, gives an impressive reading which the stooge accepts as an answer to her question. The medium then proceeds with the usual "one ahead," leaving the specially folded question until last—if the readings go that far.

On the face of it, it would seem utterly absurd to suppose that the suave Doctor Reese could have used such a timeworn gimmick to puzzle not only Thomas Edison, but such keen minds as Woodrow Wilson, Charles Schwab, Professor Hugo Munstenberg of Harvard, and many other notables whom he listed among his "clients." What seemingly ruled out the "one ahead" was the fact that Reese gave so many of his demonstrations for one person only—as with Edison— and on other occasions worked only for a small, select group, all of whom could be implicitly trusted. Never, in any of his feats, was there even a remote possibility of collusion, a fact which caused Richet and other investigators to class all of Reese's work as demonstrations given under "test conditions."

Here, again, Reese had an advantage that they never recognized; he was adept at another form of "message reading" known as the "billet switch," which consisted of picking up a folded slip, and laying it casually aside, yet in the same action secretly exchanging it for a similar slip concealed in the bend of the fingers. By cleverly combining the "one ahead" with the "billet switch" and injecting a neat subterfuge of his own, Reese consistently threw the keenest observers completely off his trail.

Here is how he managed it:

Reese would tear a sheet of note paper into several small slips that he would lay on the table so his client could write the questions and fold the slips. While doing this, Reese would secretly retain a slip for himself. When he turned away so he could not see what his victim was writing, he would fold it twice and keep it in the bend of his fingers to serve as a "dummy" slip. Even before the client had started to write the last question, Reese would interrupt long enough to gesture to the slips already folded and tell the person to keep them all to one side. In the same movement, he would switch his "dummy" for the nearest slip, toss the dummy with the others and brush them away with the back of his hand, a most disarming and unsuspected action.

That done, Reese again turned away while the client was writing out his final question. That enabled Bert to unfold the purloined slip, read it, and refold it, thus setting up the "one ahead" with a question that the unsuspecting victim had actually written! Next, again turning toward the person, Bert would repeat his gesture toward the folded slips, but without touching them, telling the person to put each slip in a separate pocket—a lower vest pocket, an upper vest pocket, a coat pocket, and so on. Here, all the eagle-eyed Bert had to do was note where the dummy slip went, and remember that particular pocket, say the upper vest.

Bert would then say, "Let me have the slip

you put in your inside pocket." He would press the slip to his forehead and would immediately read its message, much to the amazement of his client. What Bert was really "reading" was the slip he had already read and was holding in the bend of his fingers. As he finished his "reading," he switched the palmed slip for the one the person had given him, telling the person to open it and verify it. While the client was doing that, Bert turned away again and coolly opened the new slip that he had swiped, so he was all set for the next. He kept asking for slips, pocket after pocket, but he was always careful to finish with the pocket containing the dummy slip, so when he read the final question, he had the dummy back in his own possession.

Sometimes, when there was a lot of room to walk about, Bert would suggest that slips be placed in desk drawers, or on bookshelves, or other places around the room, which made it all the more impressive and also gave Bert more leeway in opening questions and reading them, since he could stroll about, too. With Edison, he asked that the questions be written in another room, but after they were brought in, they were distributed in various places, as usual, and Reese was ready with his dummy slip before that started. After secretly reading the question about the alkaline battery, Reese merely repeat-

107

ed it, parrot-fashion, when he pretended that he was reading the slip itself.

On the other occasion, Edison wrote "Keno" while Reese was present and purposely made the letters small, so that Reese couldn't spot the word from a distance. But he had no idea that a switch of slips was coming up and that Reese, while turned away, would have a chance to read the word at the closest range he needed.

But Bert's neatest twist was this: Every now and then, he would make it harder for himself by suggesting that a client write his mother's maiden name, or the ages of his grandchildren —if he had any—or something else that Reese could not possibly know. In such cases, he would often have the client place the folded slip between the pages of a book, or under an ashtray. Sometimes these were additional questions, written after the others, and occasionally, Bert would almost forget about one of them. Then, remembering it, he would have the client take the slip himself and press it against Bert's forehead. Immediately, Bert would give the maiden name, or whatever it happened to be and would then have the client unfold the slip to prove that he was right.

There was no chance for a billet switch in such a case, because Reese never touched the slip; nor could the one ahead have helped. But neither was needed. Bert simply primed himself in advance, by picking up little-known data regarding his prospective clients, then artfully inducing them to test him with it. The "mother's maiden name" was his favorite, and it began cropping up so frequently that he finally had to drop it because people began wondering why so many of his clients seemed anxious to have Bert tell them their mother's maiden name.

Another "test" that Reese overplayed, particularly in England, was having a man put a written slip inside his watchcase, the big ornate kind that they carried in those days. Reese would then apparently read whatever it said, right through the solid metal. Here, Reese had two alternatives. He could use a suggested question, like the "maiden name," or he could ask for a slip from the person's pocket and switch a palmed slip for it while telling the man to put it in his watchcase. That is, he worked the switch before the "reading" instead of after.

This created so much talk that Reese had to do it regularly and as a result, he ran into a snag when he encountered a far bigger faker than himself, the notorious Aleister Crowley, who ran a Satanic cult and claimed that he was the beast with the Number 666 mentioned in the biblical Book of Revelation. Reese really expected to impress Crowley, but while he was handing him slips and pencil the beast blandly remarked, "I've heard that you can actually read a written question that a person puts inside a watchcase. Is that correct?"

"Of course," returned Reese. "Write what you want."

"I've already written it," said Crowley. "A three-letter word here in my watchcase. I would like you to read it."

Reese couldn't and didn't, so Crowley let him go on with his regular readings. Crowley wrote questions pertaining to black arts and occult rites that were totally unfamiliar to Reese. As Crowley stated later, "He read my questions correctly, but failed to answer any of them."

That was exactly what happened with Edison later. Twice, Edison wrote words that Reese simply duplicated. A few more such "tests" would have convinced Edison that Reese's "readings" were nothing more than a mental echo, at best. What Edison wanted was to propose a mental question that would produce a mental answer, as a link between one mind and another. That was what I provided. As I have already stated, he put the question, and I gave the answer.

Now for the question that my psychic intuition tells me is in every reader's mind: How did I learn the word in Edison's mind without resorting to slip reading or verbal suggestion?

Very simply and directly. I said, "Mr. Edison, I want you to spell your word mentally, letter by letter. Just keep it in mind and go through the alphabet in order, concentrating upon the first letter when you reach it; then do the same with the next letter and so on. Ready for the first letter: A—B—C—"

There, I stopped speaking, but gave a slight nod for "D" and another for "E"; then I stopped nodding, but kept thinking through the alphabet at the same tempo, just as Edison was doing. I had my left hand on his wrist; the pencil was in my right hand. When I reached the letter "O," I wrote it down almost automatically, but I still kept thinking through the alphabet, clear to "Z," partly to double-check and also to maintain the tempo. Then I said, "The next letter: A —B—C—" This time "S" was the letter that fixed itself in my mind; and the test continued thus until I spelled out the full word: O—S—M —I—U—M.

Uncanny? Unbelievable? Neither! Most people who have witnessed my public performances have seen me utilize the same system with subjects whom I have asked to concentrate upon a word, name, or number. Frequently, I have found two persons in the audience—both entire strangers to me—who can transmit numbers directly to each other. This method dates back a full century and was once erroneously called "muscle reading," because a muscular impulse is perceptible if a person is overanxious to convey an impression.

But in the vast majority of such cases, no muscular action is either noticeable or involved; hence the term "nerve reading" is more appropriate, because at times a nervous tension is involved, which incidentally is more apt to restrain any muscular action, rather than further it. Yet nervous impulses are also absent, particularly in transmitting letters of the alphabet, where no tension whatever is involved. That is why I prefer the term "contact telepathy" which is actually what it is.

Understand, telepathy itself is seldom experienced completely on its own. On one point, I agree with Dr. Charles Richet; namely, that rather than being something "extrasensory," telepathy is a "sixth sense" in itself, hence it often works in conjunction with other senses. You can see a man fire a gun, and you can hear it at the same time, because two types of sensory impressions are involved, so no one will doubt that you perceived both. But if you should see a picture fall from a wall and immediately gain a mental flash that a friend of yours had died at that same hour, skeptics would argue that you merely guessed it, even if the impression proved correct.

A point I would like to stress is this: If Edison had written the question, "What game do I have in mind?" and put me to the test, I would have spelled out the word "K—E—N—O"—or any other game that he might have chosen, just as I did with the word "Osmium." What's more, I'm sure Bert Reese could have spelled out "Keno" if he had tried my system; but he used "nerve reading" of a different sort—sheer nerve—with so much nervous energy that he probably couldn't have stayed still long enough. He had to keep moving around, puffing at a cigar and constantly relighting it so he would have a match flame to help him read the slips he secretly opened.

I repeated this test several times with Mr. Edison and found him to be a perfect subject. I could literally sense the approach of each letter, so that when I reached it, it was like a peak, with the remaining letters showing a constant decrease. In fact, these tests with Edison did more than anything else to convince me that contact telepathy could function entirely on its own, without the aid of other sensory clues. Later, I learned the reason why it was so easy to pick up Edison's impressions.

When Edison's hearing had begun to fail him,

he found it easier to converse with some of his associates by having them tap his wrist with a pencil, thus spelling out words in Morse code, which to him was practically the same as a spoken language. Hence when I proposed to pick up letters by pressing my hand on his wrist, I was practically putting the procedure in reverse.

Incidentally, Mr. Edison told me later why he had the word "Osmium" in mind. Osmium is the heaviest of all metals and is found in platinum ore, or in combination with iridium. When alloyed with iridium, it is used in pen points and in special machine bearings, so Edison was interested in its possibilities with some of his inventions. What interested me, when I found it out, was the fact that osmium never occurs in a free state, but always in combination with some other metallic element, yet no one doubts its existence. Personally, I feel the same should apply to telepathy, in its relation to other forms of sensory perception.

FIVE

Several years before Professor J. B. Rhine began his experiments in extrasensory perception, at Duke University in North Carolina, a French scientist named Jules Romains wrote a book entitled *Eyeless Sight,* covering his studies in "paroptic vision" or the ability to "see" through sensory channels other than those of sight. His theory was that early in man's evolution, all the nerve endings of the body played a concerted part in the perception of surrounding conditions; but that later, specialized organs were developed for such senses as smell, taste, hearing, and sight.

That meant that the sense of touch, so-called, was dependent on thousands of skin centers that had perceptive powers similar to sight, but had become neglected to the point where no one was aware of their former function. To put his theory to the test, Romains began a series of experiments with persons chosen at random.

ey were blindfolded and asked to identify
jects placed in front of them. Romains found
that if they moved their hands toward the
objects, as though groping in the dark, they
were able to discern shapes and colors as well.

But they were not groping in the dark, except
for the blindfold, because the objects were in
full light; and the tests showed that the brighter
the light, the better. Further, if their sleeves were
rolled up to their elbows, thus bringing the
myriad skin centers of the forearms into play,
the results became sharper. By loosening their
collars, more "skin sightings" were provided by
the throat and chest; while some persons were
able to distinguish objects placed behind them,
but close enough to be "viewed" by the back of
the neck. A warmth, or tingling sensation frequently confirmed the various "sightings," and
the best results were gained by the nerves of the
fingertips.

Jules Romains summed up his work with the
statement: "I have taken, in the course of these
hundreds of experiments, all imaginable precautions to eliminate the smallest chance of
illusion or trickery. Any qualified investigator
can repeat them by taking the necessary trouble.
The facts which I have obtained are, without
exception or reservation, laboratory facts."

One qualified investigator who went to the

necessary trouble was Doctor Harlan Tarbell, a naprapathic physician who was also a practicing magician and the author of a comprehensive course on magic. Being naturally interested in anything that savored of the mysterious, Tarbell tried out the tests for himself and developed them into an act which he called "Seeing With the Fingertips." He included it in his combination lecture and magic show, which he presented from coast to coast.

Tarbell's act was impressive indeed. It would have particularly impressed Jules Romains, if he had seen it, but I doubt that he ever did. Tarbell invited a committee to come to the platform and blindfold him thoroughly, then guide him down the steps into the audience. There, he invited people to hold up objects just beyond the range of his fingertips, and as he groped in air, he called off item after item, all correctly, while he worked his way along the aisle.

At one moment, he would pause, lower his hands and spread them as though outlining an object by aid of radar waves. Finding it to be something "large—black—shiny—" he would finally identify it as a woman's handbag and would ask the owner to open it and hold up random articles. Always keeping his fingertips several inches away, he would make out the shape of a lipstick, describe the glint of a makeup mirror, and identify a set of car keys, which he would then take from the lady's hand and jingle for the audience to see and hear.

After correctly stating that an object was a pencil, Tarbell would take it between his thumbs and fingers, hold it up for all to see while he moved his hands back and forth along it, finally naming its color. He would repeat this with various pencils; then switch to coins, naming their value without touching them; then, by taking one between his thumb and fingers, he would give its correct date. For the benefit of skeptics who thought the raised figures gave him the necessary clue, Tarbell would switch to "something green—shaped like an oblong—a bank note!" Then, taking it between his hands, he would rub the corner with his thumb and correctly state the value of the bill. After that, by moving his sensitive forefinger slowly along it, he would call off the serial number without a miss.

If you don't think that any of this is possible, just try it for yourself. Naturally, you won't get results like Tarbell's, at least not right away. But you may be surprised how quickly your groping brings results, even though feeble. One way is to walk into a lighted room with your eyes shut and feel your way to a table or shelf that you know is there. Then pass your hands above it, preferably confining your gropes to one corner or a limited area. Another way is to enter a darkened room, where a lamp or light switch is close by the table, so you can place yourself there; but in that case, shut your eyes and turn on the light before you begin to grope.

A still better way is to have someone arrange a few random objects on a table, while your back is turned. Keep your collar high, so the back of your neck doesn't give you an inkling of what is going on; and be sure to tell your friend to put the objects in strong light. Close your eyes, work your way to the table and use the grope system. Don't try to force an impression; just let an image flow and once it is fully formed, don't try to build it further, or your imagination may run away with it and spoil the whole thing.

In short, in your first experiments, your impressions are apt to be crude and two-dimensional. For example: Someone puts a pack of cigarettes on the table; and as an afterthought, lays a packet of matches on top, set at a forty-five degree angle toward the upper right. Your impression of this would be an upright rectangle with a diamond in the center. You might even sense that the sides of the diamond were not quite equal, so that it was slightly rectangular in its own right. But if you tried to rationalize it, the combination might strike you as a playing card, surmounted by a lump of sugar. If you said that, the test would probably be classed as a failure.

So it would be better to stop where you are sure, saying, "I see an upright oblong, with a diamond in the middle—a narrow diamond, pointing up to the right corner." All of which would be one hundred per cent correct, simply because you didn't overestimate your limited impression. Later, as you get the knack of it, your paroptic imagery will take on a three-dimensional development. In the example just given, you might almost feel that the large rectangle was bulging up from the table, giving the distinct impression of a pack of cigarettes, with the diamond shaping up as a packet of matches.

There's just one drawback. Keeping your eyes tightly shut is something of an effort, which may detract from your necessary concentration. Besides, if you do score a real hit, even your best friends are apt to claim you peeked. People are funny that way. They will trust you with anything from their house keys to their credit cards; they will believe anything that you tell them, provided it is something that they personally believe could happen. But if it is something they don't want to believe, they will belittle it and will not only claim you cheated, but will even do some cheating on their own, or lie about what really happened, saying it wasn't so, if that is the only way they can find to prove you wrong.

So the best way to experiment in paroptic vision is to have your friends blindfold you to begin with, using a large-sized handkerchief, and preferably a thick one that they can tie so tight and pull so well down over your eyes that they will be positive you can't see anything. That gives you the necessary confidence to relax and proceed with the test, concentrating entirely upon the mental image that you are trying to induce. It should satisfy the skeptics, too, only sometimes it doesn't. If you're hitting well, they're apt to call it luck; and every time you miss, they'll say that proves their point. They'll hurry you, heckle you and even try to take over the act themselves, finally saying if you don't come up with real results, they may as well end the nonsense.

That's when you should begin groping a little faster and more confidently, leaning slightly over the table and opening your eyes beneath the blindfold. You'll find that if you look straight down, you can see past the sides of your nose and get a good look at the setup on the table. No matter how tightly they blindfolded you, there's no way of preventing you from getting that needed glimpse. In fact the tighter, the better, because you can keep scowling while they tie it, as though it really hurts. That brings your forehead muscles down beneath the handkerchief; and when you're ready for that "looksee" past your nose, you merely have to arch your eyebrows good and high, so that the blindfold goes up with them. Later, you relax the forehead muscles and down it comes. Just like shifting gears in a modern automobile transmission. It's automatic.

That's how Tarbell did it. Even though he was "sold" on the idea of eyeless sight and could hit a remarkably high percentage every time he tried to legitimately, he couldn't "sell" it to an audience in that form. When people pay to see near-miracles, they want near-miracles, not just good guesswork. And Tarbell's "Seeing With the Fingertips" looked miraculous when he used his special blindfold. He put squares of surgical gauze over each eye and held them in place with strips of adhesive tape slanted outward on each side of his nose. He stretched another adhesive strip straight across to hold the works in place. Over that went the handerkerchief, tied in back like a regular blindfold. Trickery seemed impossible, yet Tarbell used the method as described. He kept his eyes shut and his brows downward during the taping; and after the handkerchief was in place, the usual lift of the forehead muscles drew the tapes up with it, far enough to allow the downward peek.

The hundreds of Tarbell students still active in magic may be surprised to learn that he actually believed in "Eyeless Vision," as he sometimes termed it, but he couldn't afford to make it public, because he felt that magicians generally would write him off as a "nut" or accuse him of selling out to the spiritualistic crowd, who were still smarting from the lacing that Houdini had given them and therefore eager to find a scapegoat. But he confided in me, because he knew that much of my work was genuine, too, and therefore I would understand. Not only that, he gave me a demonstration of his real eyeless vision, under conditions which I can guarantee were airtight and the results were phenomenal. I could also name a few of Tarbell's close friends who would say the same, because he confided in them as well and backed his claim as he did with me.

The one question we all asked him was where he found time to practice the genuine work, being busy as he was with his lecture tour and writing new material for his correspondence course. He had the right answer for that, too. He reminded us that during his regular demonstration, he would occasionally hesitate before describing an object and that almost always, he took his time when naming colors. The reason was, he actually kept his eyes shut until he formed an impression of an object or a color. Then, before naming it, he took a quick downward peek to see if he was right, and if he wasn't, he simply changed his call.

By keeping mental count of his "hits" as opposed to "misses," Tarbell was literally testing his actual ability with a "live" audience, but nobody suspected it. So he was able to note how his average improved and sometimes, when impressions came quickly and sharply, he would take a chance on them, knowing that if he happened to miss, he could concentrate, gain the necessary peek, and give the correct answer. But he insisted that he seldom missed in those cases, and I was inclined to agree with him. The point that impressed me was that nobody ever put over a good copy of Tarbell's act, any more than they have mine. When you're in the big money, as we both were, and imitators keep dropping by the wayside, it's proof that you have something they don't have.

One performer tried "Seeing With the Fingertips" and lost out because he overplayed it. That was Rajah Raboid, a great showman in his own right, who put on one of the best crystal gazing acts in the business. For a publicity stunt, Raboid decided to put on the "fingertips" at a publishers' convention. Wearing a full beard and attired in Hindu regalia, complete with turban, he visited various booths and allowed himself to be blindfolded. Opening a book at random, he held it so that committee members could see the page and watch him run his finger along the lines, calling each word aloud as he touched it. Presumably, his educated fingertip was picking up the printed type as easily as if it had been stamped in braille.

The Rajah was doing a good job, too, for he was using a thick blindfold that would have given many performers a lot of trouble where fast reading was concerned. But he had it fixed so that it overlapped his turban, which had hidden hooks in the lower edge. The hooks took hold and when Raboid adjusted his turban, a very natural move, he had only to give it a slight backward tilt, and it brought the whole blindfold up automatically. Afterward, he pressed it downward by reversing the process. But the trouble was, the act was too good and too repetitious.

The committee began figuring there must be some gimmick for Raboid to be so letter-perfect, and the Rajah couldn't switch to other tests—like naming objects and colors—as a throw-off.

So as Raboid was nearing the bottom of a page, a smart skeptic suddenly grabbed a large advertising placard from a booth and thrust it between the Rajah's blindfolded eyes and the book, blocking any possible view. That would have discommoded ninety-nine mind readers out of a hundred, but Rajah Raboid happened to be the one in a hundred. While moving steadily along each line, word by word, he had been reading on to the end of the page, just to be ready for any unfamiliar words that might appear there.

So in his smooth, confident style, the bearded mystic went right on to the finish, which should have squelched the skeptics completely, except that as already stated, he was playing it too strongly. He knew the words all right, but since he couldn't see them, he went badly out of line, even "seeing" a word at the end of one line when it belonged at the beginning of the next. That "gave away the gizmo," as they say in the trade, and from then on the field was left pretty much to Doctor Tarbell, who went on seeing with his fingertips until he finally retired.

So the "know-it-alls" charged it all off to trickery and went on imitating Tarbell's act inadequately, until within recent years, a Russian girl named Rosa Kuleshova began confounding scientists by distinguishing colors, pictures, and finally reading printed words with her fingertips, even when heavily blindfolded. This started in the Ural mountains city of Nizhniy Tagil, and soon twenty-two-year-old Rosa became known as the "Miracle Girl of Tagil," launching a tidal wave of popular enthusiasm that carried her to Moscow on its crest. She was tested under laboratory conditions at the Soviet Academy of Science, and her work was pronounced genuine.

That really opened the floodgates. Russians galore began reading with their fingertips and statistics were compiled indicating that one out of six persons could distinguish colors by the sense of touch, with the ratio of sensitivity much higher among children. As a result, "child wonders" began springing up all over Russia, performing new sensations such as seeing through solid objects and giving the scientists a merry whirl of it, until skeptics spotted kids peeking from under eye masks or over the top of black-lensed goggles. Even Rosa lost face when she claimed she could read a book by simply sitting on it.

But the results of the extensive color tests still were classed as official. Many persons were not only able to "feel" the colors, but to describe the sensations that they induced. Some colors were smooth, others rough, and stickiness was also an

identifying factor. These and other features
followed reasonably consistent patterns, which
gave the Russian scientists a chance to establish
theories regarding "skin sight," just as Jules
Romains had done some forty-odd years before.

But oddly, nobody gave any credit to Jules
Romains, even though many of his tests had
involved blind people, which became the rule
in the Russian labs as well. Nor was there any
mention of Harlan Tarbell, who had put on
public demonstrations of the very type that
Rosa Kuleshova was to copy years later. Tarbell
was gone by then, but Romains, still active in
his eighties, was prompt to remind scientists-at-
large that credit for the discovery of eyeless
sight belonged to him. To that, Tarbell would
have echoed full agreement, had he been
around to do so.

The business of "beating the blindfold" goes
back long before eyeless sight. Whenever fakery
was involved, it was naturally smart to insist
upon a blindfold in cases where it wouldn't
hinder the performer's work. That, however,
could prove to be a boomerang, when a blindfold was really a handicap; hence the "peek"
came into vogue. Take contact telepathy as an
outstanding example.

Here, one of the most impressive tests is the

finding of a hidden article, by simply picking up nerve impulses from a person—or persons— who knows where it is and keeps his mind concentrated on that fact. Obviously, the telepathist, as "receiver," must concentrate even more strongly than the "sender" and can actually do it better when blindfolded, being free from outside distractions. Once guided to a spot where an object is hidden—such as a letter under a sofa pillow—it is easy to feel about with one hand, while holding the sender's wrist with the other.

But once you expand the field of activity, by hiding an article outside of the room where the test is taking place, or even putting it in another building, or somewhere outdoors, you can get lost while on the way from one place to another, as the "impressions" are fewer and more difficult to interpret. This became evident back in the horse-and-buggy days, when Washington Irving Bishop, the greatest contact telepathist of his time—and perhaps of all time—cooked up a publicity sensation known as the "Blindfold Drive." A committee would hide an object anywhere in town; then they would blindfold Bishop, help him aboard a wagon and join him there. He would take the reins, slap the horses, and they would go larruping down the street, around corners, on a mad chase that would

wind up at the chosen destination, where Bishop would order the committee to help him to the
sidewalk to continue the hunt.

From there on, it was a matter of routine. The
problem lay in the drive itself. The performer
had to be blindfolded, or he could have watched
the reactions of the committeemen, or even
picked up signals from people in the crowd,
confederates who might have snooped around
to learn the chosen destination. By slowing the
pace and keeping close contact with the committeemen, it would have been possible to pick
up guiding impulses; but that would have
spoiled the show.

Rivals sprang up to compete with Bishop, and
they all found that the hell-for-leather drive,
with excited crowds dashing alongside, was the
only way to rouse the public to such a fever
pitch that they would pack the local opera house
to witness the mind reading show that evening.
So the performer had to use the blindfold peek
for two reasons: First, to find out where he was
to go; and second, to keep track of where he was
going after he took off on his mad race.

One of the best ways of handling the first
problem was this: After being blindfolded, the
performer would ask one of the committeemen
to concentrate on the route he had in mind,
suggesting that he should trace it with his

forefinger, either on a table or in the air, as if using an imaginary map: "One block north along Main Street—then another—then a block to the right—left at the next block—" and so on. That would be the sample suggested by the performer, so while the committeeman traced the actual route in similar fashion, the performer would tilt his head back, press his hand dramatically against his forehead and try to pick up the imaginary impression.

He picked them up all right—by glimpsing the committeeman's hand and counting the blocks. A neat device here was to have one committee member do it for the benefit of another, so they could both concentrate on the same course, rather than think of different routes to the destination. Off they would start and while driving the wagon, the performer would again tilt his head back and get a peek at each street corner, so he would know when to jerk the team left or right. True, his view was limited, but it was usually enough; and to increase it, the performer would often drive the team standing up, not only allowing himself a wider range of vision, but giving the wild drive the spectacular touch of a Roman chariot race.

All that went out with the horse and buggy, but the act itself was still good. By then, vaudeville had come into vogue and was popular in big cities, in contrast to the days when such shows had played the tank towns. So the newer version was for the mentalist to start from some advertised place like a hotel entrance or the theater lobby, where he was first blindfolded, then walk along between two committeemen, pressing one hand against one man's wrist and his other hand against the other's shoulder.

Now, this looked like the regular contact act, or "muscle reading," but actually it wasn't. In working on a stage, or even moving out among the audience, you can pick up impressions so subtle that you can't identify them as such. I'm speaking of personal experience when I say this and at the same time discounting the way some bunglers practically shove the committeemen around, which naturally ruins the act. But when you're walking down the street, blindfolded and with a committeeman on each arm, you can't go shifting around at every corner, trying one direction, then another. Even though you're after a subtle impulse, the committeemen may begin to resist so obviously that it looks like you're shoving them around when you aren't.

That I also learned from experience and with it, the right way to do it, so smoothly, so neatly that even the committeemen are totally flabbergasted. Upon nearing a corner, you peer down from beneath the blindfold to stop at the proper spot. Then you simply wait, motionless, telling

132

your companions to keep concentrating. No sway, no push. In fact, you're practically at a dead center, which could mean a long delay before picking up an impression, and that could be bad, too.

So while you wait, you keep looking down from under the blindfold, watching the feet of the committeemen. No matter how calm and immobile they try to be, in surprisingly few moments, one or both of the committeemen will turn his foot in the direction you are to take. In effect, intense concentration produces a subconscious reaction, in which the man literally, yet inadvertently, points out your path. The moment that you get that wigwag, you go, drawing your companions along with you, much to their amazement. If neither points his foot, after a due pause, you simply continue straight ahead. When the trail gets really "hot" as you near the chosen address, you will find that the pace is slowing, so from there on, you work it like a door-to-door canvass, stopping long enough to watch for another foot twitch. When you spot it, you know that you are there.

That's the way it should be done. In contrast, I'll describe how it shouldn't be. Just another case of how a good act can be ruined by a poor performer, but very funny when I look back, although it didn't seem so then.

There was a small-time vaudeville mind reader who called himself Professor Newman, the Great "Magic." He worked blindfolded, mostly with stacked decks, one after another, doing practically the old Pinetti act, but if anyone insisted on shuffling the cards themselves, he would switch to a routine involving the blind-fold peek. Oddly, his act, crude though it was, went across fairly well, because he was such an eccentric character that he always managed to cover up his failures by switching to something else.

Understand, this was not George Newman, a famous mind reader who had once featured the blindfold drive and continued on for many more years, doing feats of mentalism that deserved top rating. But I have an idea that the "professor" had heard of his more famous namesake and wanted to emulate him, or that some booking agent had gotten them confused.

Anyway, somebody arranged a publicity stunt in which Professor Newman was to do the equivalent of a blindfold drive—namely, the "blindfold walk" that I have already described —in the very heart of Manhattan, starting from Grand Central Station, no less. A committee was to seal an object in a small package and place it, somewhere in the area, and the professor was to find it, blindfolded, under the strictest test conditions. The stunt was so well publicized

134

that reporters and cameramen showed up, bringing a correspondingly large crowd, and the eccentric professor suddenly found himself on the verge of fame.

Now, either Professor Newman had never heard of the foot pointing system, or had never used it and was afraid to try it. All he knew was the blindfold peek, and what he wanted to know was the name of the place where the package had been planted. So he took a chance that was so bold, it was really good. There he was, all blindfolded, with the committeemen ready to go and a crowd gathering in Grand Central, and he still hadn't learned the one fact he had to know. He turned toward one committeeman and then the other, saying, "You are sure you know where the package is? So I can exercise the mind and find it!"

Both said they knew and wanted the professor to start out, but he shook his blindfolded head, and said, "No, no! You must be sure! Is there a telephone book near here?"

There was one, on a stand beside a handy phone booth, but the professor pretended not to know it. He asked them to take him to it, and he pawed until he found it, then turned to the man on his right and said, "I want you to do this. Open the book to the name of the place and put your finger on it, so that your friend here can see. Say nothing, just point to the name, and he can nod that he is sure. No whispers—nothing! It's just that two minds must think the same."

So the committeeman on the right opened the book and pointed out the name to the man on the left, while the professor, squeezed between them, kept his hand to his forehead, saying, "I must exercise the mind!" while he peered down past his nose and saw the name: MENDEL'S, in large black type.

That was all he needed, especially when he saw a number on Forty-second Street as the address. At that time, Mendel's was an all-night restaurant down the street from Grand Central, and a popular meeting place for vaudeville actors when they came in from late dates in such places as Stamford and White Plains. Having this information, Newman turned away, purposely blundered into the corner of the phone booth, reached out his arms so the committeemen could find them and headed for Mendel's.

Naturally, he took the long way around, bumping into the information booth, starting through a train gate, and finally going out to Lexington Avenue. At times, the committeemen were holding back, subconsciously trying to steer him correctly. At other times, they were giving him leeway, but he paid no attention to that. Watching his own feet, he worked his way

back to Forty-second Street and sped his pace as
he practically dragged the committeemen into
Mendel's, with reporters, photographers, and
some of the crowd following. Next, he was
blundering among the tables, shoving chairs
aside or looking under them, and when the
committeemen began steering him toward the
door, he went behind the cashier's counter,
poking underneath for the all-important package. When it wasn't there, he knew it must be in
the kitchen, so he headed that way, pushing the
manager aside when he tried to raise a protest.

By the time the professor was rummaging
among the pots and pans, the police arrived and
hauled him out through the back door. He had
lost the committee somewhere along the way,
and he hadn't found the package. When he
pulled off the blindfold and found the committeemen, they were telling the reporters just what
had happened, and everybody was having a big
laugh, though it took the professor quite a while
to understand why.

In hiding the package, the committee had hit
upon a smart idea. They figured that the blindfold stunt might create some turmoil around
Grand Central. To keep the whole thing close to
home, they had checked the package at the
terminal parcel room, which in those days—
back before the era of coin lockers—did a very

thriving business. One man had the check for the package with him, and they'd arranged with the clerk to let Newman through, so that he could ramble around until he found it.

It seemed like a real tough test for him to pick the right package out of a few thousand, but actually the committee would have done the work for him, though they didn't realize it. They knew the number of the check, and the shelves were all numbered in rotation, so the professor would have had it cinched from the moment the clerk opened the gate.

But he never got that far, because at that time, the commodious parcel room at Grand Central Station was leased as a concession, though very few people gave any attention to the fact, thinking that they were dealing directly with the New York Central or the New Haven Railroad. The name of the company operating the parcel service was Mendel's, and their address, like the restaurant, was also listed as Fortysecond Street. Professor Newman had picked the wrong Mendel's, the only one he knew about.

SIX

Among persons claiming the power of x-ray vision, Joaquin Argamasilla was a real standout. A youthful member of a wealthy Spanish family, he convinced European scientists and psychic investigators that he could actually "see through" certain metals, preferably gold or silver and to some degree with other metals, though they were apt to give him trouble. Argamasilla came to New York in 1924 and began to put on demonstrations of his uncanny ability, which promptly brought him into conflict with Houdini. At that time, Houdini was stepping up his campaign against fraudulent spirit mediums in order to publicize his forthcoming road show, which was to feature spirit exposés along with an evening of magic.

Personally, I have always felt that Houdini "jumped the gun" where Argamasilla was concerned. At no time did Argamasilla claim supernatural power, which was the only type of deception Houdini ordinarily denounced. But Houdini never hesitated at stretching a point that might prove to his advantage, and the Argamasilla case cropped up at a time when he needed all the publicity he could get. Otherwise, it would have been better for Houdini to let the Spaniard with the x-ray eyes build himself up into a supersensation, so that the exposure of his methods would have gained still bigger headlines.

Yet I say this with due reservation, because it is quite possible that if Argamasilla had really reached the peak he sought, he would have been a jump ahead of Houdini and thereby could have continued his x-ray demonstrations under test conditions that would have nullified Houdini's explanations. I have reasons to suppose that Houdini recognized that; and if so, he could very well have decided to nip the Argamasilla business in the bud, before it got out of hand. That would have been in keeping with Houdini's constant policy, for he was always an opportunist. So the best way to cover the subject is from Houdini's own description and analyze it from there.

Argamasilla was a tall, amiable, good-looking chap who worked under the direction of a manager. He used an oblong silver box, with a hinged top, which was secured by a small padlock when closed. A printed card or a written slip of paper was placed in the box beforehand. When the box was handed to Argamasilla, he gripped it with one hand at each end and chose a position with the light behind him and the spectators in front, facing him. All the while, he guarded against observers being at his side or behind him. This, according to Houdini, enabled Argamasilla to release a turnbuckle near the left end of the box—the padlock being near the right end—and thereby push the lid a trifle upward with his thumb, thus secretly getting a peek at the card inside the box.

The silver box measured about $9\frac{1}{2}$ by $2\frac{1}{2}$ inches, with a height of 2 inches. Argamasilla also used another box with approximate dimensions of $7\frac{1}{2}$ by $3\frac{1}{2}$ inches, with a height of about $2\frac{1}{2}$ inches. This box had grooves at the ends and one side, so that lids of different metals—copper, zinc, tin, and iron—could be slid in place, thus subjecting Argamasilla's vaunted x-ray vision to comparative tests. Each of the sliding lids had a projecting flange that corresponded with another at the center of the box, enabling the lid to be padlocked there. In this case, Houdini claimed that each lid was flexible, so its front edge could be pressed

upward and the grooves were oversized, allowing further play, which produced a narrow
space through which Argamasilla could peer.

But it still wasn't all that easy. Try it yourself
with some printed business cards and a metal
file case, raising the lid just a fraction of an inch.
You won't need x-ray vision, but unless you can
slide the card to just the right position and get
the light at a perfect angle from above you, you
will find that you will have to read in the dark,
which is every bit as difficult. So after explaining the method so neatly and so satisfactorily,
Houdini decided to settle that trifling question
with the following statement:

> "Reading of the card is made possi-
> ble by variable deflection of both light
> rays and visual beam, and by proper
> manipulation of angles, the eye has a
> range of practically the full bottom of
> box from front to back walls; the card
> being kept in left hand corner of box.
> By turning the box upside down it is an
> easy matter to slide the card out of box,
> enough for reading, and even at that it
> can be obscured from observation by
> the onlooker by the angularity in posi-
> tion of holding box."

142

Quite an afterthought, that final sentence. It means that when you find that the explanation was wrong, you switch to another that doesn't fit the circumstances at all. In the original description of Argamasilla's x-ray demonstrations, there was no mention of his turning either the silver box or the box with sliding cover upside down, for several very good reasons. First, Argamasilla claimed to be reading through metal, so the card was obviously placed with its printed side upward and the box would necessarily have to be held that way.

Next, if Argamasilla had kept tilting the box from one side to the other, or turning it forward and backward until he finally managed to invert it, the space between the lid and the box would be away from him, so he couldn't slide the card out toward himself where he alone could see and read it. Instead, he would be sliding it out away from himself, and everybody else would see it.

The alternative would be to turn the box deliberately upside down, by switching the ends to the opposite hands, thus bringing the opening your way, but the process would be so obvious that it would rouse immediate suspicion. Therefore Houdini certainly should have mentioned it at the outset; but he didn't. So the

143

obvious conclusion is that Argamasilla never worked it that way with his own boxes. Such handling of the silver box would have been bad enough, but a turnover of the box with the sliding cover, never. For if Argamasilla had inverted that box, he would have deliberately contradicted his own claims. Remember, it had interchangeable covers of different metals, to prove the penetrative power of his gaze and whether he could see more easily through copper than through zinc, or tin, and so on. Hence turning the box upside down would have nullified the whole procedure, limiting him to reading through steel alone.

How, then, did Houdini suddenly become sold on the notion of turning the box upside down to get at the contents? The answer to that question is found elsewhere in his account of Argamasilla's doings. Houdini first witnessed a few of the gifted Spaniard's demonstrations, and thereupon jumped to his original—and inadequate—explanation of a simple "peek," which was frequently his way of doing things. So for his next test, Houdini brought along some boxes of his own, and challenged Argamasilla to try his penetrating gaze on those.

One was a tin box put out by a well-known candy company. It had a hinged lid and ordinarily contained nuts and fruits. Since there was no lock to the box, Houdini provided a large elastic band to put around the box, but had purposely chosen and tested a band with enough slack for Argamasilla to thumb the lid upward and gain a peek inside. He let Argamasilla handle the box with the band around it, long enough for the Spanish marvel to recognize its weakness. Argamasilla agreed to use that box, which immediately roused Houdini's suspicions, because the lid and the sides were heavily covered with painted decorations, chiefly black and gold. Now, from the very start, Argamasilla had specified that he could work only with unpainted boxes, which gave Houdini a chance to brand him as a phoney. But first read exactly what Houdini said:

"Notwithstanding the ban that Argamasilla puts on painted metal, he did accept this box for a test, and safely so, because a casual examination shows the lid securely hinged, but the means of holding lid closed is so elastic that the manipulation made necessary became identical with that for the silver box; however, Argamasilla took precaution to turn box upside down to facilitate reading."

In short, Argamasilla was *not* using the same manipulation as with the silver box which he *never* turned upside down. Nor did he violate his own rule against painted boxes, as Houdini insisted he did. Look at any fancily decorated candy tin, and you will see that the bottom is *unpainted*, since it is never on display. So the only way that Argamasilla could use the box that Houdini brought was by turning it upside down. He may even have said so and *insisted* that the card be placed with its printed side down, because he *intended* to turn over the box. If so, those were details that escaped Houdini, the man who could escape from anything.

You ask why? With all due respect to Houdini, simply because he was sure that Argamasilla was a faker and that gave Houdini the right to "explain" Argamasilla's methods any way he wanted, whether correct or not. The trouble was, the explanation had to be convincing; and the business of playing peekaboo under the box lid had its weak points. So Houdini brought along his own box, expecting Argamasilla to handle it as he had his own, only not so smoothly. Instead, Argamasilla really crossed things up by using an entirely different technique. Houdini caught on to the turnover method, which Argamasilla may have improvised for the occasion and to even the score, he used it to

146

bolster his shaky explanation of Argamasilla's handling of his own boxes.

Actually, it is highly doubtful that Houdini guessed right in the first place. My analysis is that Argamasilla needed something much surer than a peek in the dark and certainly wouldn't have tried to baffle scientists as well as Houdini unless he had something a lot better than that. Sliding the card out through the slit was adequate; I'll go along with Houdini on that and give him credit for spotting Argamasilla's moves with the tin candy box. But with Argamasilla's own boxes, no. He would definitely have had no reason to turn them over.

That leaves one plausible solution that Houdini completely missed; namely, that each of Argamasilla's boxes was gimmicked so the printed card or written slip would slide into sight, as needed, but at the bottom of the box, not through the space between the cover and the lid. Actually, that was nothing new. Such a gimmick dated back to Professor Anderson, a Scotch magician who thrived some eighty years before Argamasilla's time. Anderson, who styled himself the "Great Wizard of the North," put on a second sight act, demonstrating what he called the "transparency of opacity," in which he identified objects placed in a special mother-of-pearl case, which for some miraculous reason succumbed to the power of his penetrating gaze.

A more modern form of such a gadget consists of an oblong box of Japanese construction in which blocks of various colors are placed and concealed beneath a hinged lid, much in the manner of Argamasilla's silver box, the main difference being that the Japanese box is made of wood. A highly important difference, because the box lid has a special panel that can be pushed upward, disclosing a narrow slit that runs the full length of the box, thus showing the colors of the blocks within, enabling the performer to call off their order. Cheap versions of this device have been sold by novelty shops in recent years, but the original apparatus was so finely made that it could stand close inspection and could be automatically locked at the conclusion of the demonstration, rendering it absolutely foolproof.

Now Houdini was a great gadgetman himself, with all his escape boxes and their special panels; his milk can with its sliding collar; and so on. But Argamasilla still could have bluffed him into thinking that the x-ray boxes depended upon manipulations only, because the young Spaniard presented another baffling test which seemingly eliminated any possibility of gimmicks. He would ask for a hunting case watch, the type with a hinged metal front that protected the crystal and would let a person turn the hands while the front was closed.

Meanwhile, Argamasilla allowed himself to be blindfolded, with wads of cotton for his eyes and a folded handkerchief over that; then, taking the watch and raising it to eye level with the front toward him, he would name the exact time at which the hands were set. This fitted perfectly with his claim of x-ray vision, for hunting case watches—which men still carried in those days—were usually gold or silver, the two metals through which Argamasilla claimed to see most easily. He regretted that he could not look through from the back, because the steel works of the watch were so thick that they obscured the hands. Hence, only a watch with a hunting case could be used in the test.

Repeatedly, Argamasilla put on this demonstration with uncanny precision, raising and lowering a watch until he found the exact angle suited to his x-ray vision. But here, again, Houdini argued that he was using a peek method. He claimed that Argamasilla invariably stood back in a corner close to a window, to get better light, and swept his hand downward to waist level, at the same time secretly opening the front of the watch case a mere half inch. Yet that was enough, for by bringing his hand close to his body, he could work the old trick of looking down beneath the blindfold and spotting the time shown by the hands.

Here, again, a sharp angle of vision figured, but the light was in Argamasilla's favor, since his gaze was downward, and he also knew exactly what to look for; namely, the position of the hands on the watch, which was much easier than trying to read printed or written words. But, before accepting Houdini's explanation as final, one particular statement should be noted. Referring to one of Argamasilla's demonstrations, Houdini declared:

"I had opportunity for standing at his extreme left side and from that position *I positively saw him open and close the watch.* Of course, he did not know of my vantage point, because of his blindfold, as I looked over his left shoulder."

Now, in the pamphlet in which that account appears, Houdini also included a chummy photograph of himself with Argamasilla, when they were still on speaking terms. Houdini was short, and even though he edged somewhat forward, as was his habit in such photographs, the picture plainly shows that Argamasilla was more than half a head taller than Houdini. How Houdini could have looked downward over Argamasilla's shoulder without first climbing on a chair, is as big a mystery as some of Houdini's famous escapes.

Again in due deference to Houdini, he probably guessed correctly regarding Argamasilla's action; but the point is, he only *guessed* and did not *see,* as he claimed, because, from his own description, that would have been physically impossible. What he could have seen was a betraying action on Argamasilla's part, such as shifting the watch to a better position just before the downward sweep. But such a move can also be a "throw-off" to mislead a sharp observer, particularly when the performer has some better method at his disposal, as I have reason to believe that Argamasilla had.

Houdini stated that on one occasion he gave Argamasilla a watch that was hard to open and that the test failed that time. Also, Houdini claimed that he personally practiced opening and closing a watch in the manner described and was able to sight the time without observers detecting the move unless they knew the trick beforehand. Yet at no point in his analysis did Houdini cast any suspicion on the watches used, beyond the fact that they had to open readily. Argamasilla could have used his own watch, or his manager's, or one that had been planted with a supposed stranger, and Houdini would have adhered to his explanation, just as he did with the boxes, for Houdini had no objection to Argamasilla using his own boxes.

Remember, Houdini only explained the reading of the cards in the boxes, but never demonstrated it. But with the watch test, he not only explained it, he was sure he could do it. Often, since then, I have wondered what would have happened if the chips had been really down, and Argamasilla had challenged Houdini to duplicate the watch test, for a sum like $10,000, with the proviso that both would work in slow motion, with witnesses placed at every angle, ready to call "Stop!" at any moment. Houdini could very well have lost out, because several years after Argamasilla abandoned his brief career as an x-ray visionist, word began spreading among mentalists about a specially imported gimmick that could produce a minor miracle. It involved an old-style hunting case watch, which could be set at random, yet the owner couldn't miss when it came to naming the time. To me, that was an immediate flashback to Argamasilla, and once I acquired one of the rare watches and tested it, I was convinced that this was either the secret that Houdini had guessed at, but missed, or something every bit as good.

To all appearances, the watch was perfectly normal, and the stem could be turned to set the hands anywhere while the front of the case was open. When closed, the cover locked neatly in place, but could be released and opened by pressing the stem, as with any standard watch of that type. But when the cover was shut tight, it did something more than just lock. It engaged an inner ratchet that controlled the stem-winder so that after a few turns, the setting apparatus ran entirely free, without moving the hands at all.

To start, the demonstrator turns the hands with the case open, or lets the spectator do so, then tells the spectator to close the case and turn the hands as much more as he wants, so they will be set entirely at random. Thus for the demonstrator to name the time would require either x-ray vision, as Argamasilla claimed, or a clairvoyant faculty, as a modern mentalist would put it. Now, actually, the farthest that the hands can turn is to a specific limit known to the demonstrator. For instance, if the hands are beyond 12:10 when the case is closed, the limit of their turn would be 2:18. Once past that, their next stop would be at 3:56; past that, at 5:24; and so on.

So instead of trying to sneak a peek after the case is closed, the glimpse is gained beforehand, when it apparently doesn't matter. If the time should be 3:05 on the watch, that would mean 3:56, which the performer has memorized as one of his "keys." If he has a long way to go, he can close the case himself and give the stem a few turns before handing the watch to the spectator and telling him to do the same, making sure that the spectator will keep turning the hands well past the limit where they set themselves. Also, the demonstration can be repeated indefinitely, with no fear of detection.

Assuming that Argamasilla was equipped with foolproof boxes and a surefire watch, why should he have bowed out so suddenly? Simply because soon after Houdini barged into the scene, Argamasilla's manager, a Brazilian named Davis, realized that the going would be too tough from then on. Only a few years before, Houdini had shied away from exposing fake spirit mediums, because he was afraid that public protests by believers might injure the vaudeville bookings for his escape act. But during the interim, he had switched to making serial movies with himself as the hero, and when they had begun to flop, he had started antispiritualistic campaigns in the towns where the serials were showing, hoping to give the box-office receipts a shot in the arm.

In addition, Houdini had begun to bait mediums, denouncing them personally as frauds;

and to counterbalance that, he had hired some vaudeville mind readers to appear in person at the movie houses where his serials were showing. That was really playing both ends against the middle, and Argamasilla was caught squarely in between. The fact that he had baffled scientists by trickery made him fair game for Houdini's attacks, and since Argamasilla had no status as a vaudeville artist, he couldn't accuse Houdini of unfair action toward a fellow member of the craft.

There was a real touch of irony in that, for some years previously, Houdini had used the Zancigs as a mind reading team with his own magic show in England; and Sir Arthur Conan Doyle had pronounced the Zancigs' act as genuine, just as other notables agreed that Argamasilla had x-ray vision. But that was before Houdini started on his antispiritualistic campaign and furthermore, Julius Zancig, the male half of the team, apparently had some gift of foresight, for he had been smart enough to join the Society of American Magicians, which habitually elected Houdini as its perpetual president. If Argamasilla had known all that, he might have joined, too. As it was, with Houdini practically stealing the show, his best policy was to bow out, which he did. No more was heard from him from then on.

At least, Argamasilla was ahead of his time.

Houdini died a few years afterward and so was no longer around to challenge a new mental marvel, who came up with the same claim of an ability to see through metal, but far more effectively than Argamasilla. This new possessor of x-ray vision was a veteran of World War I, who had been blinded by a terrific flare from a bursting shell. Eventually, he had regained his sight and with it, the fantastic ability to see through metal, much like Argamasilla. Indeed, this newcomer could very well have been borrowing a leaf out of the Spaniard's book, because his fantastic faculty functioned better with silver than any other metal—except, of course, gold. But his technique was entirely different.

No boxes were involved, nor did this new marvel read time on closed watches. Instead, he had people place two silver dollars directly in front of his eyes, fixing each in place with adhesive tape, so firmly that there was no play whatever, nor any chance of seeing past the edges of the coins. Various objects were then held in front of him, and he identified them by means of his penetrating gaze. Like Argamasilla, this man had a manager. In fact, he specially needed one, because ordinary daylight bothered him so badly that he could scarcely see his way around, but once it was filtered through the

eighth-inch thickness of the silver coins, his
vision improved accordingly.

Naturally, chicanery was suspected, as it always is with any sort of marvel, no matter how
genuine or legitimate it may be. In this case, a
code seemed the most plausible answer, but no
communication—either spoken or silent—could
be traced between the manager and the demonstrator, and any other persons suspected of
collusion were gradually cleared. Still, the code
theory persisted, until the man with the x-ray
sight completely spiked it by driving a car
through the city streets, slowly of course, but so
convincingly that it was obvious that he must be
operating entirely on his own.

Just when and how the secret leaked is still
uncertain, but it presumably resulted when
some sharp skeptic noted the date on one of the
silver dollars and provided himself with one
exactly like it. Afterward, he artfully managed to
switch his own coin for the one that had been
used in the x-ray demonstration. When the
purloined coin was put to the test, skeptics
found, somewhat to their amazement, that they
could actually see through the metal, but in a
most unusual way.

A needle-thin hole was drilled directly
through the center of the coin, the opening
being so placed that it would take a microscope

to detect it in the design of the coin. But when placed directly in front of the eye, the tiny aperture provided a complete view of the immediate scene and a remarkably clear one. To prove it, take a postcard, punch a hole in it with a pinpoint and hold it close to your eye. You will see everything within a reasonably limited circle and the closer the "blindfold" to the eye, the greater the circle of vision. A simple law of optics, this, but whoever thought up the coin caper was smart, because nobody would ordinarily have linked the two conflicting factors of the solid metal blindfold and the pinhole view.

Once the secret spread, imitators began duplicating the stunt, but by then it didn't matter. Blindfold drives had attained such popularity that nobody had to talk in terms of x-ray vision any longer. Performers could call it clairvoyance, yoga, mentalism, psychic power, or a new form of radar control, and the public would be just as happy. No need for silver dollars or such gadgets, any blindfold would do, provided it was handled in convincing fashion. The blindfold drive had been exciting enough in the old horse-and-buggy days, but the horses at least could see where they were going, even though the driver might be goading them hell for leather.

But for the driver himself to pilot an automobile through city traffic while fully blindfolded was a highly spectacular twist. As Nick Kenny, the columnist, said when he heard that a lady mentalist was scheduled for a blindfold drive, "It's bad enough for women to be driving cars at all, let alone doing it blindfolded." Actually, some blindfold drivers have run into complications with state authorities, who have questioned their right to renew an operator's license if they intend to use it in so irregular a manner. One wonder-worker came all the way from India to New York City, intending to drive a car blindfolded through Times Square, but he failed to impress traffic police with his prowess and had to settle by riding a bicycle blindfolded instead.

Even that might be difficult to arrange today, but if you can talk the local authorities into letting you drive a car or ride a bike blindfolded, your next step will be as follows: Obtain a large handkerchief, at least 18 by 18 inches. Almost any material will do, provided you can see through it when you hold it toward the light, but the thicker or more opaque it seems, the better. Therefore, a dark-colored handkerchief is usually best. Lay the handkerchief flat on a table, with one corner pointing away from you. Then, beginning with the inner corner, start rolling it loosely toward the center. When you arrive there, switch to the far corner, and do the same thing, except you will be rolling it inward instead of outward.

With a little practice, this becomes more of a folding process than a mere roll and by bringing the upper half squarely down upon the lower, it makes eight or more folds or thicknesses of cloth in all. Have a person place this over his own eyes and hold it there while you tie the ends tightly in back of his head and he will agree that it forms a thorough blindfold. Even if he can see a trifle downward, that will be no help, because to navigate through traffic, a person has to see straight ahead.

After letting anyone try the blindfold to his own satisfaction, spread it out again and roll it as you did before, but when you place it on yourself, turn your hands forward, so that instead of the folds being directly in front of your eyes, the crease is placed there, thus separating the two divisions. This makes the blindfold wider, so that it looks all the more formidable, but when it is tied in place, it can be spread still further, so that there is only a single layer of cloth before your eyes. You will find that you can see through this quite readily.

That's all that's needed for a blindfold drive, but other measures are frequently adopted. Powder puffs placed over the eyes can be thumbed aside when drawing the blindfold tight. Special blindfolds are also made with fixed folds that prevent any visibility until flipped in the proper direction, when the blindfold is reduced to a single layer, or opens at a seam, only slightly, but enough to look through. Some of these devices are very ingenious and are supplied to the trade by dealers in such props.

You don't even need a special blindfold, if you work with a cloth hood, as many blindfold drivers do, provided of course that the hood itself is gimmicked. In adjusting the hood in place, it is a simple matter to push the blindfold up around the forehead, so that it no longer covers the eyes, but can be drawn down again before the hood is removed, so that the blindfold appears to be intact.

That means that the performer only has to look through the hood, which has a thin layer of cloth in front and a thick layer in back. When the performer puts the hood on somebody else, he turns the thick layer to the front, so that the person cannot see through and therefore assumes that the performer is similarly handicapped when wearing the hood. Here, again, some neat devices have been introduced, such as a hood with a thin spot that can be found easily, if you know where to look for it, but practically never, if you don't know where to look.

By practically never, I mean just this: Any competent performer should know how to size up a committee and handle them accordingly. Otherwise, he shouldn't be posing as a mentalist. If using an ordinary blindfold with a trick hood, the performer should bait an eager committeeman by giving him the blindfold to examine and handing the hood to someone else. By the time the eager beaver wants to look at the hood, it has already been examined to the committee's satisfaction, so there is no reason to delay the act.

Of course, there is one way to put a blindfold driver to a real test. Don't worry about the blindfold, or the hood, or whether he can penetrate silver dollars with his gaze. Ask someone to provide a metal pail or bucket. Fill it with water and let it stand long enough to prove that it doesn't leak, which means that there are no holes in it. Empty it and put it upside down over the head of the prospective blindfold driver. The drive will be postponed indefinitely, because nobody can look straight ahead through an unleakable pail or bucket.

That, however, will not prevent the downward peek from beneath an ordinary blindfold. So a good showman could still put on an act of "seeing with the fingertips," as Tarbell used to do, or an adaptation of the watch reading demonstration put on by Argamasilla. There would be no need to use a hunting case watch; any open-faced watch would do, since the x-ray vision would apply to the metal of the bucket. Either way, the performer goes about actually groping for objects, but keeping his hands low, so he can bring things that people give him into his range of downward vision.

From there, he raises the objects to eye level or above, purportedly piercing the metallic bucket with his all-seeing gaze, the really dramatic punch being provided at that moment. Above eye level is better, as it helps keep the bucket balanced toward the back of his head. Otherwise it might flip forward beneath his chin when he does his next downward peek, which naturally would not help the act.

SEVEN

One phase of ESP that always provokes controversy is the supposedly chance factor of "thought coincidence." In the early days of telepathic tests, persons acting as "senders" would draw pictures of almost anything that came to mind, and others serving as "receivers" would try to duplicate them. Naturally, there were lots of misses, and any results that came even slightly close were regarded as evidence of something.

To eliminate such uncertainty, special tests were introduced, most notably the type adopted at Duke University, where two persons operate with identical sets of twenty-five cards bearing five different symbols. One person goes through his set, thinking of each card that he turns up, and the other tries to match the cards mentally. There are quite a few variations of this test, but that one example will suffice, as it establishes the general purpose—namely, to learn if "hits" can be made consistently on an average better than the chance expectancy of five out of twenty-five, or one in five.

Such results are regarded as evidence of extrasensory perception, but critics of the tests argue that it is still nothing more than chance. What if someone does hit eight, nine, ten, or even fifteen or twenty out of twenty-five, time after time? Somebody else may be hitting only three, two, or even none, which counterbalances the situation. The law of averages allows for such freakish extremes, but when you do hit, which is it? Thought transference? Or thought coincidence?

One man who had the answer to that question was Thomas Edison. He summed it in a single word: "Both." In short, it might have been telepathy; yet at the same time, it could have been chance. Get two minds thinking alike and they will become attuned, so to speak, and the same thought chains will follow. That was why Mr. Edison insisted that I repeat tests in which he concentrated upon certain cards, names of places, or lists of his inventions. The results were phenomenal. I called them off as correctly as if he had spoken them aloud. But Mr. Edison was not surprised, not in the least.

He told me that he had similar experiences with some of his associates who had worked with him in developing his new inventions. Often, he would be struck with a sudden idea and would send for a man to discuss it, only to have him arrive brimming with enthusiasm over practically the same idea, even though Mr. Edison had not yet mentioned it. What impressed Mr. Edison most was not that he and his associates should think alike—he expected that —the perfect timing was the significant factor, as it connoted both thought transference and thought coincidence.

That raised the possibility of a "controlled coincidence," in which thoughts of various persons could be combined to produce a planned result. I said it would be quite possible, but only with persons whose minds were attuned to a common objective. However, I added that such a test could be simulated with any group; but that it would depend on an ingenious device, rather than any actual form of ESP. When Mr. Edison said he would like to see such a test, I proceeded with it, as follows: I brought out an ordinary pack of cards, had someone give it a thorough shuffle and hand it to Mr. Edison, to whom I said, "I want you to count off a small number of cards—any number up to a dozen—and put the cards in your pocket. Remember the number, but don't tell anyone what it is."

With that, I turned my back, and after allowing due time, I turned to Mr. Edison and continued, "To make sure you remember the number, I want you to count off the same number again. This time, square the cards in a little packet—" as I spoke, I indicated the action with my hands"—and look at the bottom card. Remember it and replace the packet on the pack."

While Mr. Edison was doing that, I turned to three other men who were present and told them, "I want each of you to think of a girl's name and keep it in mind, without mentioning it to anyone else." Then, after another pause, I said to the first man, "Now, take the pack from Mr. Edison and deal cards one by one in a little pile, a card for each letter in the name that you have in mind. I'll turn my back, so tell me when you finish."

When he said that he had dealt the cards, I told him to pass the pack to the next man, so that he could do the same. Then I told the second man to pass it to the third, who also spelled the name that he had chosen.

All the while, my back was turned and when the third man announced that he had finished his deal, I told them, "Good. Now that you each know exactly what to do, I want you to put your cards back on the pack." Over my shoulder, I

gestured in the direction of the first man, saying
"Yours—" and then the second, "Yours—" and
the third, "And yours." As that was done, I
continued, "Now hand the pack to Mr. Edison
and ask him to add the cards that are still in his
pocket, so that you can proceed with the full
pack."

That was done and I turned toward them for
the first time. Since Mr. Edison had the pack, I
asked him to pass it to the first man, so he could
count out the cards to spell the name that he had
chosen, exactly as he had before. I had him pass
the pack to the second man, who spelled his
chosen name and passed it to the third, who did
the same. I told the third man to push the next
card face down from the pack, so that it lay
isolated on the table. Then I stated, "Mr. Edison
has not told anyone his number; nor have
the rest of you mentioned the names you have in
mind. I assure you that I have no idea what card
Mr. Edison looked at, and at no time have I even
touched the pack. If I should name his card, you
might say it was telepathy or clairvoyance, but
to have the card reveal itself, would be something more: thought coincidence. Would you
kindly name your card?"

To that, Mr. Edison replied, "The six of
hearts." To that, I bowed and gestured to the

lone card on the table, as I asked, "Would you mind turning up the card yourself?"

He turned it up. It was the six of hearts!

Oddly, when analyzed, this thought coincidence can become all the more baffling, as its apparent simplicity causes observers to overlook one seemingly slight but highly essential detail. In effect, one person—in this case Mr. Edison—counts off the same number of cards *twice*, in order to verify it. Thus, if his number happened to be ten, the card he looked at should have been number twenty from the top of the pack, after he added the first ten from his pocket.

Now, if the other three participants had chosen the names MARJORIE (eight letters), CLAIRE (six letters), and ALICE (five letters), the total 8 + 6 + 5 = 19 would have hit it right on the button. In fact, I always asked those participants to state the names they had in mind after the card was turned up, just on the chance that it did hit on the button. Once in a while, it did. When it didn't, it came so close that it not only had them guessing, but wondering. I mean wondering if the Amazing Dunninger could have hypnotized them into spelling a name with one letter more or less, as ANN or ANNE; or even JEAN or JEANNE. They might have wondered, too, if I could have palmed a few cards on or off the pack—except that I never touched the pack from start to finish!

Figure that out yourself! Take any pack and follow the procedure exactly as I have described it and see where you wind up. You will find that the chosen card reveals itself automatically, every time. Edison's number could have been four instead of ten; the three names could have contained any number of letters, yet the result would have been the same.

The gimmick is this:

In dealing cards to spell a name, letter by letter, each card is dealt on the one before, thereby reversing their order. Simple and natural though this is, it sets up the climax.

For example, suppose the original person counts off four cards and puts them in his pocket; then counts off another four, notes the bottom card and puts the packet on the pack; and that three persons, A, B, and C choose the names SALLY, IRENE, and MARY for a total of $5 + 5 + 4 = 14$ letters. That puts the noted card (say the king of clubs) the fourth down from the top in a group of fourteen cards. When those fourteen cards are spelled and replaced by A (5), B (5), and C (4), thus reversing their order, the noted king of clubs will be fourth up from the bottom in the group of fourteen, putting ten

cards above it. When the original person re-
places the four cards from his pocket on the
pack, they make up the difference. The noted
card will have fourteen above it and when the
names are spelled as before, the next card will
be the king of clubs.

It just can't miss, provided you make sure that
the three spellers reverse the cards as they deal
them. I made sure of it in Edison's case by
performing a few preliminary tests in which I
had people deal cards one by one, so they were
conditioned to the "reverse deal" when I came
to the demonstration of thought coincidence.
But there is another way which is absolutely
foolproof, though the effect is not quite so
spectacular. That is to have the three people (A,
B, C) call the names to start, so that you can
explain how they are to spell them.

As soon as the original person has noted the
bottom card of the packet that goes on the pack,
you turn to him, take the pack, and ask for the
three names. Once they are announced, you say,
"Very good. Now I want each of you to spell the
name you gave me, one card at a time, like this."
With that, you turn toward Mr. A. and draw off
the top card with your right thumb, letting it
drop on the right fingers; then draw off the
second card, letting it fall on the first, and so on,
as you spell: "S-A-L-L-Y."

With only a momentary pause, you turn to Mr. B. and continue to draw off cards, letting them fall on those before as you spell "I-R-E-N-E." Finally, you turn to Mr. C. and do the same with "M-A-R-Y." You then say, "That's all there is to it, so take the pack and spell the names yourselves, by dealing the cards on the table. But wait!" As an afterthought, you turn to the original person, and say: "You still have some cards in your pocket. Add them to the pack, so it will be complete when these gentlemen spell out the names that they selected."

That clinches it and from there on in, it is all in their hands, giving it the impact of an impossible coincidence. It doesn't matter in what order they spell the names the second time, as the noted card is just where it should be!

Whenever I am asked, "What do you regard as the simplest, most direct demonstration of ESP?" I reply without hesitation, "'The Three Card Test.'" I say without hesitation, but not without a certain reservation. Namely, I prefer to call it an experiment in telepathy, because I devised it when I was appearing at the famous Eden Musee on Twenty-third Street in Manhattan; and that was long before I had heard of ESP. In fact, nobody had ever heard of ESP, because the term was not coined until fifteen years later.

My test was simplicity itself, because I used playing cards, with which everyone is familiar, and I limited the choice to three, thus avoiding any confusion. With all due respect to the Duke University experiments that began fifteen years later, their special symbols cards made it almost impossible to gain spontaneous results. But I can't be smug about any discovery on my part since I hit upon the "Three Card Test" quite by accident.

I was working an old-time card trick in which the name of a selected card was to appear on a blank slate, and to make it easy, I was using what magicians call a "one-way forcing pack" in which all the cards are alike, an item that audiences seldom suspected in those days. Later, for the "Rising Card Trick," I used a three-way pack, composed of three different cards arranged in continuous sequence, so that no matter how much the pack was cut—but not shuffled!—you could spread it and invite a person to take three cards in a clump, or cluster, and he would be sure to draw the three you wanted.

I had taken on a new assistant, and what did he do, but switch the forcing packs. I showed the blank slate, set it on a stand and had a spectator take a card, which should have been the ten of clubs. With the one-way pack, I could shuffle before and after, which I did quite nonchalantly; and as a final touch, I turned to the table and gave the pack a riffle. I saw the ends as they dovetailed and caught a glimpse of red along with black, I knew then that I had the wrong pack —the three-way, comprising the six of clubs, eight of hearts, and queen of spades.

In a spot like that, a magician couldn't publicly blame his assistant for what he'd done. So I gave the pack another riffle and indignantly told the man, "You didn't bother to look at the card you took, did you?" There are times somebody does forget to note a card and thereby ruins a good trick. On that particular occasion, I was hoping it was one of those times, so I could drop the slate trick and go on with something else. But, no, the man said he'd remembered it and from the way he grinned, I knew he hoped I couldn't find it.

That gave me a quick idea. I turned the pack toward myself, fanned it, pulled out a six of clubs, without showing it, and told him, "If you're really thinking of your card, this is it. But you're trying to bluff me by thinking of another, like this one"—with that, I pulled out an eight of hearts, without showing it; and then, after a moment's hesitation, I pulled out a queen of spades and added, "Or maybe this one."

With that, I laid the pack aside, as if it were

ordinary and didn't matter. I had no idea which card he had taken, but it had to be one of those three, so I decided to fluff it off with that, as three guesses out of fifty-two would be a highly convincing average. So I walked up to the spectator, spread the three cards in a wide fan, turned them toward him at eye level so that other folks could see them and announced, "You see your card there. Am I correct?"

He hesitated a moment, then nodded and said, "Correct."

But in that moment before the nod, I saw his eyes move to the right of the fan and fix there, on the six of clubs. Taking the cue, I turned the cards in my direction, whipped away the two odd cards and ordered, "Name it!" When he responded, "six of clubs," I snapped it face front toward him. I'll never forget his look nor the applause that followed. The slate trick couldn't have touched it.

I worked another trick instead of the "Rising Cards" and after the show, in order to bawl out my assistant properly, I spread the shuffled three-way pack and told him to take a card so I could shuffle it back in. I worked the same routine and watched his eyes as I had the spectator's. His fixed on the queen of spades and that was it.

Soon, I was working the trick for backstage

visitors between shows, without telling them it was a forcing pack. One day when I stopped in Martinka's Magic Shop, somebody who had heard about the trick wanted to see it, and rather than give away the fact that I needed a special pack, I took three cards from an ordinary pack, spread them, and said, "Think of one." It worked as the other trick had, but better. Since this spectator was mentally choosing a card, his eyes fixed more keenly and all I had to do was name it. I repeated it, using different cards, for half a dozen customers who were in the shop. It knocked them for a loop and I went my way, thinking I had a real good trick.

It still had bugs, however. First, I found it needed a buildup to be effective. So after a card was chosen mentally, I put all three in my pocket, then drew out two slowly, without showing them and finally said, "That leaves your card. Name it!" When the person did, I'd bring the card from my pocket, and it would prove to be the right one, because I always took care to note the position of the card on which the person fixed his eyes and keep it in my pocket as the last one.

Then I would start over with another person; and still another, always with each group of cards going in the pocket. Normally it should have kept building stronger and stronger, except that it didn't. I soon found out why. This was different than taking a card from a pack. When asked to select one of three, mentally, some people were more spontaneous than others, especially after they watched the way the others reacted. Instead of fixing on a card, they'd give the fan a casual glance, then look away and say, "All right, I've got one," leaving no clue as to which card it was.

I soon discovered how to handle such customers. Whenever I saw an eager beaver coming up, I would start the fan toward myself, then spread it wider as I turned it toward the spectator, inviting him to note a card, which I already was doing. That way, I carried his glance along with mine and by making the desired card a trifle more conspicuous, I would literally "force" it on him as a mental choice.

Now, this takes practice, but when tried repeatedly, it is by no means difficult. The right thumb is in front of the fan and does the spreading, but the left fingers should travel along the outer edge of the fan, as though to adjust it—which it does—and thereby it provides the subtle touch. The front card of the fan shows its entire face and is therefore the most conspicuous, which means that a casual observer is apt to reject it.

So if you want him to take it, the best plan is

to spread the fan wider, as though to stress the others, even pushing the front card farther with the left fingers. This carries the spectator's eye along and suggests that he should choose that card, even though it is still the most conspicuous, because it is rendering the others more conspicuous than they were before.

But where does that leave the middle card, if you want it taken? If you spread the others, the spectator will shy away from it. So don't spread the others, except maybe very slightly. Simply push or draw the middle card outward, showing enough more of it to encourage the spectator into picking it, which he usually will. As for the card at the rear of the fan, you can make it the natural choice by pushing both the others outward or bringing it inward with your left fingers. The more neglected it looks, the better it works.

All this is good psychology, but perhaps you are wondering what it has to do with parapsychology, which covers ESP, etc. Just this, as I kept working the test, I found I could work it automatically, coming and going, so to speak, without watching the person at all. I would take the three cards, give them a quick fan toward myself and get a flash impression of the one that impressed me most. Then I would close the fan, turn it toward the subject and spread it in exactly the same way, saying, "Think of one of these cards—just one—do you have it?"

If his reply of "Yes" was prompt, I would go by my flash impression, treating it as a thought projection that he had picked up. If he proved slow in response, I took it that he hadn't caught my flash impression, but had formed one of his own, which it was my job to pick up. That meant that instead of my being the sender, I was the receiver, so I would act accordingly, by again turning the cards in my own direction, spreading the fan exactly as before and making a deliberate choice to pick up his projection.

Generally it was different; occasionally it was the same. But I seldom had it miss in such cases. Overall, I hit the ninety per cent correct average that I have consistently maintained in all my demonstrations. This is not a guarantee that you can do the same; but you will certainly hit far above the thirty-three and a third per cent of mathematical expectancy. If you don't, you aren't telepathic, that's all.

That's a fact you have to face. There are color-blind people who drive through red lights thinking they are green; and others who are tone deaf, who can't tell one musical note from another, so it is not surprising that many should lack the ability to transmit or receive thought impressions. From my own experience, I have

179

found that suitable subjects run about seventy per cent. So with the "Three Card Test," if I didn't pick up a thought impression, I would go on to someone else.

That meant returning to the nontelepathic person and giving him a flash, or following his glance, as already described. If you're using that system anyway, you're all set to start. But you can still encounter trouble from a couple of other sources. Somebody may not like the cards you show him and will insist on taking three of his own, then nursing them so you don't get a glance at them. Even worse, some smart customer may change his mind after taking a card, just to crab your act.

Suppose you've shown him the queen of clubs, three of hearts, and five of spades. You're sure he's picked the three of hearts, which he actually has. You put the cards in your pocket and bring out the queen of clubs and the five of spades, naturally without showing them; and as you reach in your pocket to draw out the three of hearts, you say, "Name it!" and he says, "Queen of clubs." You know he's lying, but where does that leave you? It leaves you wishing that by some miracle, you could bring out the queen of clubs instead of the three of hearts, to prove that you could outsmart him despite his chicanery.

Actually, you can do just that, without resort-

ing to the miraculous. Here's how: Before working the "Three Card Test," secretly plant two
extra cards in your pocket. Now, you proceed as
usual, letting someone take one card out of
three, putting them in your pocket, bringing out
the other two, then his. You show them all, drop
them on the pack and turn the pack face up, so
you can take out three other cards to show to the
next person.

Keep doing this until you come to a tough
customer, one you're sure may try to outsmart
you. Just don't worry which card he picks. Note
their order as you put them in your pocket, as:
three, five, queen. Now, in this case, you pick up
the pack and hold it face down in your left hand
before your right begins drawing cards from
your trouser pocket. Deliberately you draw out
one card, saying, "This isn't the one you're
thinking of." Put it on the pack and do the same
with the next. You're telling the truth, because
those cards are not his at all. They are the two
that you planted in your pocket, so you still
have his three cards there.

So you're still telling the truth, when you say,
"That leaves your card in my pocket. Name it!"
Whichever he says—three of hearts, five of
spades, or queen of clubs—you draw it out, top,
middle, or bottom, as the case may be, and show
that you hit it right. Put it on top, turn the pack

face up and draw out three more cards for the next person to choose from. You just can't miss when you use this system; and what makes it all the better, you are ready for a repeat, with two cards in reserve for anyone else who tries to outguess you.

If you want to win your audience's confidence and build up your own, you can use the two extra cards at the start, keeping the pack in your left hand all the time and placing the extra cards face down upon it as you bring them from your pocket. That way, you can hit the first four or five tries "on the button" and take chances after that. In taking those chances, you actually show the other two cards after bringing the chosen one from your pocket; and any time you miss, you can tell the person that he didn't concentrate enough, so you will test him with three other cards. Since you still have two extras in your pocket, you can switch back to the "surefire" system on your second try. Just don't overdo it to the point where somebody may become suspicious.

EIGHT

Long before ESP cards were invented, mentalists were presenting a twenty-five-card test utilizing ordinary playing cards, chosen at random from a standard fifty-two-card pack. Five different persons are given five cards each, told to look at them and remember one card from the group, then shuffle it. The demonstrator then gathers cards singly from each participant, thus mixing them still further. Next, the mentalist spreads groups of five cards before each person, telling them that anyone who sees his card is simply to concentrate on it. One by one, the participants do just that; and in each case, the mentalist draws the correct card from the group!

Now the remarkable thing about this demonstration is that it can be done three ways—through telepathy, through psychology, or through chicanery. That certainly offers a wide range of choice, yet in each case, the procedure is so similar that even the keenest observer would be unable to detect the difference, unless acquainted beforehand with the method involved. In short, a test which comes just about as close to real mind reading as anything could, can actually be duplicated by anyone at practically the first trial.

That, in itself, is sufficient reason for ignoring the exaggerated claims of self-styled mentalists who suggest their own tests, impose their own conditions and bow out of the picture or jump on to something else before anyone has time to challenge them to repeat their demonstrations under more rigid rules. For proof of this, read, on, and learn for yourself!

Rather than give five persons five cards each, it is better to use thirty-six cards, giving six each to six persons; or still better to use forty-nine cards, giving seven each to seven persons, so I shall describe the test accordingly. In presenting it, I gather the cards singly but haphazardly, and give the pack a brief shuffle, turning it face up to show that the cards are well mixed. Then I deal off the top seven and fan them with the faces toward the first person, telling him that if he sees his card, to concentrate on it and note its position when I turn the fan face down, with my right hand.

At no time do I even glance toward the person. All I do is run my left hand, fingers

184

downward, along the perimeter or outer edge of the face down fan, slowly, back and forth, in a repeated semicircle. When working with a person who is a sensitive subject, I invariably find that if my left hand lowers during this process, as if attracted by a certain card, that will be his card; and I pick it out with complete assurance.

By complete assurance, I mean just this: In all my mental demonstrations, I have advertised that I will be ninety per cent correct, and I have lived up to that claim for a mere fifty years. But in this one particular test, I have been one hundred per cent correct, for the simple reason that it just can't miss. You either get it, or you don't. If there is no attraction, I know that his card isn't there, unless—as may happen often— he isn't concentrating sufficiently, because he isn't sensitive enough. Whichever the case, I go on to the next person, showing him the same fan of cards, so that he can concentrate on his card if he sees it; and so on, person by person.

After finding one chosen card, I continue on to the next person, on the chance that two or more chosen cards happen to be in the same group. Naturally, after finding one out of seven, I have an advantage with the next person. If his card is in the fan, the odds are reduced to one out of six; and if I score another hit, they drop to one out of five. But that, in turn, means groups in which there are no chosen cards, which may slow the process badly. A person may try to concentrate on the card he has in mind, even though he does not see it; then give it up, realizing it must be in another batch. This causes an impression to blow hot and cold, taking too much time to weed it out, though I always can as soon as it diminishes. But going on to the next person too soon, means coming back for another round, which also is a time taker.

So rather than have the audience walk out, or turn off the TV, which they often do with performers who give boring demonstrations that lack entertainment value, I prefer to start with a positive "Yes" or negative "No," and go on from there. As I spread a seven-card fan toward a person, I turn my head the other way, and say, "If you see your card, tell me so, but nothing more." If he says he sees it, I proceed as already described; if he says it isn't there, I go right on to the next person, with no time wasted on negative reactions or lukewarm impressions.

Impartial observers who have watched me demonstrate this test invariably agree that some extrasensory faculty is involved, with telepathy the primary choice, because it represents an actual action and reaction of mind upon mind.

What is more, I have convinced the toughest skeptics as to the reality of this test by letting them try to work it themselves. The results are almost sure to exceed chance expectancy and sometimes go so far beyond that people begin to feel uncanny; but there is an important point for beginners to remember here.

You may have trouble following the curve of the fan with your moving hand, or find that the cards are too close together for you to be sure just which card is causing the attraction. In either case, deal the cards in a face down row on the table, with an inch or so of space between them. Check with your subject to make sure that he remembers which card is his; then run your hand slowly along the row, several inches above the cards, back and forth, back and forth, always going to the extreme end, before reversing direction. When your hand begins to dip repeatedly, with no effort or desire on your part, signifying one particular card, that will be it.

The reason I incline toward the telepathic theory in this case is that there is no contact, no visual clue, no auditory reaction necessary; just high-powered concentration, with results in definite ratio to the amount of mental effort—or I might say, mental energy—created by the person who chose the card and is therefore trying to transmit its position to you, as receiver.

I say "position," because the cards should always be kept face down, never face up. If they were face up, another factor would arise—that of the receiver trying to probe the mind of the sender, hoping to learn his likes or dislikes in regard to certain cards. There are tests of that type, but they fall into a different category.

With this test, there is another factor that shows that something more than the ordinary senses is at work. Often, a person serving as receiver is unable to notice how his hand dips over one card in the row, and therefore he is ready to give it up as failure instead of the success it really is. This happens with some of the best receivers, because, having put themselves in a receptive mood, they are entirely oblivious to outward occurrences. So when showing such persons how to perform the test, I always station an observer at one end of the table to watch the receiver's hand from that angle. If the receiver gives up, the observer can almost always point out the right card which the receiver indicated without consciously recognizing it.

That covers the telepathic phase; now to consider the same test in terms of applied psychology. To all appearances, it is exactly the same. You gather cards singly from persons who have each selected one out of seven, mix the entire batch and deal off a packet of seven, showing it fanwise to different persons. You ask each if he sees his card and if he says "Yes," you turn the fan face down, run your hand along the edge and finally draw out the mentally selected card. Not only that, you can find it much faster, in fact, almost instantly!

Here, I can divine the question now springing to the reader's mind. "If the test is done exactly the same, how can the result be faster?"

The answer is, it isn't exactly the same. Read the two versions over and perhaps you will see the difference. If you don't, here it is: In the telepathic test, I specified that "at no time do I even glance toward the person." Later, I stressed that with the further statement, "As I spread a seven-card fan toward a person, I turn my head the other way." Now in my description of the psychological version, both those statements are omitted. I said that to all appearances the test is exactly the same, but actually it isn't. You don't turn your head away, and you not only glance at the person, you catch his glance as well.

In asking, "Do you see your card?" and receiving the reply of "Yes," you add the usual admonition, "Then concentrate on it." As he does, you note the direction of his gaze, in relation to the fan. It's much like taking aim over a gunsight, with his eyes as your target. Keeping the fan almost directly in front of you, you will see his eyes fix momentarily on the upper left corner of a card; and that will be the card he has in mind.

Here is a curious factor that there is no necessity to explain, because the fact that it works is all you need to know. He is looking at the *faces* of the cards, so he is actually fixing on the upper *left* corner of his card; namely, the index corner. You are looking at the *backs*, so to you, that would be the upper *right* corner. Nevertheless, you do your sighting on the upper left corners as you see them and note the one that seems to catch his gaze. Try it with some one and see for yourself.

Now, instead of picking his card in a hurry, you can turn your head away the moment that you have gained your sighting and then proceed with the usual maneuver of running your free hand above the face-down fan. Often, not one person will note the difference in procedure and realize that you have found the card psychologically through a visual cue, rather than telepathically, or through some other extrasensory means. People to whom I have explained this psychological method have often asked me if I ever use it in my own demonstrations, and I reply, "Most certainly—and for very good reasons."

For one, I merely claim the ability to read people's thoughts, without specifying the precise process involved. The psychological test just described is actually thought reading through the aid of a visual clue, so it qualifies. Another reason is that it is the sure way to deal with a skeptical or uncooperative person who is apt to balk or start changing his mind when I am working along purely telepathic lines. I have an uncanny way of spotting such people and by spotting a chosen card from an initial glance, I have it all clinched beforehand. Many times I have felt a skeptic deliberately trying to pull my hand mentally to the wrong card; and when I come up with the right one, you should see the amazement that follows. From then on, I can always turn my head away without a glance toward persons who are fixing their minds on their cards, and doing so in honest fashion, in a spirit of true mental cooperation.

Finally, I am a skeptic in my own right, and becoming more so in this era where people are so eager to believe in ESP, PK*, psi phenomena,

---

*Photokinesis: the act of exerting a mental influence upon a physical object, such as wishing a pair of dice to come up with a seven, while they are still rolling—and having them do so.

and all the additional trimmings that have been concocted as icing for the cake, that they are willing to accept anything as evidence to prove such claims. As a result, they not only fail to differentiate between telepathic impressions and sensory clues, they are ready to accept many forms of simple trickery as something bona fide.

Taking the "Seven Card Test," as just described, you can produce practically the same effect automatically, with no chance of failure—and no skill or intuition—by proceeding as follows: Let each person choose one card from his seven, then mix his cards face down, so that nobody knows just where his own card is. You go the rounds, taking one card from each person in regular order, saying, "I shall gather all your cards at random—."

Hold it, while we analyze that statement. You are gathering *single cards at random*, but you are taking them from *groups in rotation*. You continue thus until all have been gathered; then you remark, "Remember, you have shuffled the cards yourselves, so that neither you nor I can know where any card may be. So I shall deal them again at random, seven cards at a time—"

Here, you deal off the top seven, counting them one by one, keeping them in that order, as you add, "So I can show them to each of you and ask one simple question: Is your card there?"

You show the batch to the first person and if the reply is "No," you go on with the next, and so on. If all say, "No," you toss aside that group of cards and deal off the next seven, to begin again. But if the first person says, "Yes," you're in. You can run your hand around the edges of the fan, as if working it legitimately; but all you really have to do is finish at the extreme left, from your viewpoint. You draw out the card that you find there, show it dramatically to Person Number One and announce, "The card you have in mind!"

Continue with the rest on the same basis. When Person Number Two sees his card in a fan, you know it is second from the left. For Number Three, it will be third, and so on. Picking the chosen card is as easy as shelling peas, perhaps easier, but the harder you make it look, the stronger the effect. A neat touch is to shift the cards in a group before you fan it. If you move three from top to bottom, two from bottom to top, one from top to bottom, the first person's card will be third from your left when you spread the fan, so you start your count from there.

When I am asked if I have ever used this

193

automatic method, my reply is, "Certainly. Otherwise, I would not be so familiar with its working." But I always add that I have never presented it as a demonstration of thought reading. I have shown it only to psychic investigators, students of psychology, and other interested persons to illustrate how a valid test in telepathy can be so closely imitated by a simple trick that even an acute observer cannot distinguish between the genuine and the counterfeit.

That is the great objection to the methods of the modern ESP laboratories. In recognizing the real as opposed to the fake, they have regarded them as opposites, thereby overlooking how closely they may mesh. They want to hold tests on their own grounds, under their own conditions, because they are afraid that if they go elsewhere and meet someone else's terms, they may be hoodwinked. It never occurs to them—or if it does, they have remained silent on that score—that if they are incapable of detecting outside fraud, their own security measures may be inadequate.

That is why skeptics claim that students who register high scores in ESP laboratory tests may be taking advantage of some flaw in the procedure, but in such cases, the burden of proof rests with the accusers. Mere opportunity for fraud does not mean that it was perpetrated, or even recognized by the persons tested, particularly when they have been chosen because of their integrity. There is no reason why accredited experimenters should cheat in a parapsychological laboratory any more than in a physics lab or a chemistry lab, where honesty is automatically accepted. Taking that hard line, every advance in science could be disputed on the ground that some mischief-maker must have sneaked some foreign element into a test tube.

I still hold to the opinion that high scores registered by persons regularly tested under established laboratory conditions may result from their becoming conditioned to the process, so that their reactions become spontaneous. Their intensity of interest may induce a concentrated state in which they subconsciously pick up trifling signals without recognizing them as such; or it may represent an actual breakthrough into the realm of extrasensory perception. But when an outsider walks into a college lab and begins piling up a high box score that makes it look as though the ESP tests had been hand-tailored to his order, I have doubts as to the validity of such results. This has been going on so long that I could cite numerous cases where people have proclaimed themselves to be self-appointed ESP specialists; but they can best be summed up by taking the recent example of a so-called Swedish sensitive or psychic, Olof Jonsson, who has been eulogized in an entire book by Brad Steiger.

According to his biographer, this remarkable mystic can do quite well when he entertains a group of strangers with his ESP tests, but his more advanced phenomena require extended meditation with a group of friends. Now this, in simple terms, represents the essence of fakery. Both from long observation and extensive experience, I have noted that anything can happen among friends, which rules out such experiments or at least classifies them as nonevidential. In all my tests, I specify that I am working with total strangers, and I insist that they testify to that effect. I have time and again—as witnesses will verify—turned down a positive telepathic flash, because it has come from someone whom I know.

Not that you can't work ESP tests with your friends. Actually, they are often the best subjects, so that is the right way to begin. Home circles have served as the proving grounds for some of the most elaborate experiments in telepathy and kindred subjects and should therefore be given due recognition. But they offer a great chance for monkey business, as well. That's where fake mediums got started in the old days, and even now, smart kids start tossing objects about the house in a surreptitious fashion, scaring their parents into thinking that poltergeists are at work. It's always easy to fool your friends, because they wouldn't be your friends unless they were willing to go along with you to some degree. In addition, some friends are apt to go all out and not only brag about the stunts they see you do, but exaggerate them to the point where they sound like miracles. That's the way Brad Steiger did with the parlor tricks his friend Olof Jonsson performed.

The difficulty in tracking down these second-hand accounts of near-miracles is that usually they are so poorly reported that essential clues to the *modus operandi* are totally overlooked. Anybody who has read a magic dealer's catalog will immediately recognize this. They whet the buyer's appetite with all sorts of fantastic claims that prove to be irrelevant once he receives the real secret for which he sent in his money. Now, that's the way Steiger's book on Olof sounds, like a section on mental effects from a magic dealer's catalog. Only he's not likely to supply the secrets, not at any price, because he probably doesn't know them. So in all fairness to Brad, who honestly thinks the tests are real, I shall have to reconstruct them in equivalent form, to show how they could be done and therefore probably were done. The problem is to find a good starting point, some stunt that is obviously so hokey that it reflects upon the rest.

Now, fortunately, there is some good reporting in the book, chiefly concerning some of Olof's claims or comments on specialized tests that were mentioned in passing as self-evident proof of his psychic powers. Steiger took these so literally that they crept into the book without embellishment, thus giving us a key to what Olof could have gotten away with, without having to try very hard. In fact, for a starter, let's take a test that a bright six-year-old child could put over, without the need for preliminary practice.

Steiger, apparently convinced that Olof could "get into" a person's subconscious, asked if he could get into an animal's subconscious as well. To that, Olof blandly replied that he had done it many times. He said that in one "test," as he termed it, he concentrated on a cat and made it do many different things, such as going from one corner to another, licking its left front paw, then scratching its ear, and so on. He added that most cats or dogs respond to telepathic direction, but some do not. A very wise addendum, as that covers occasions when the trick fails to work.

When I read about this cat caper, it immediately rang a bell, so I looked up some books on simple magic that I remembered reading many years back. In one, published in England, in 1930, I found the following:

A TRICK WITH THE CAT

When you have given an entertainment and your audience is still asking for just one more, suggest that as a change from conjuring, you will ask the cat to wash itself.

This is quite easily done. Stroke the cat affectionately, at the same time asking it to wash. When you walk away from the cat, everyone will be surprised to see that it immediately does as you have asked it.

This is a capital little joke and the first time I saw it done, the joker quite convinced his audience that he had some strange power over the cat.

Here is the secret. He just took a tiny piece of butter and smeared it in the palm of his hand. If you will do this and then stroke the cat, you will find that he will immediately commence his ablutions even without being requested to do so.

Since the book sold for only two shillings and had a wide appeal, it might have been translated into various languages, including Swedish. But whether or not Olof ever read it or even heard about it, this certainly reduces what one author calls "telepathic direction" to the status of what another author styled "a capital little joke."

Of course Olof's act, as Steiger describes it, is a little more elaborate, but it presents no complications. Instead of a tiny dab of butter smeared on the palm, you use two, one on the tip of your forefinger, the other on the tip of your thumb. You can pick them up from a small pat of butter in an envelope tucked in your coat pocket. You don't really stroke the cat at all, but just start to do so, touching it lightly behind the ear with your forefinger and lowering your hand so that your thumb grazes its paw while passing it. You can draw attention from those actions by snapping the fingers of your other hand in a somewhat imperious fashion, which will cause the average cat to retire to the nearest corner, as if following your mental command.

There, it will realize that it has been buttered up, so it will respond to your spoken directions to lick its paw and scratch its ear, exactly as it does—and probably still will do—for Olof. I say "spoken directions," meaning that you speak them to the people present, so they will know

200

what you are telling the cat mentally. Being a strange cat, they should know that it couldn't possibly know what you are saying. Yet I say that with reservations, because there are people who are ready to believe in anything, like some authors.

Getting back to authors, Brad Steiger cited Olof as causing the psychically controlled cat to move from one corner to another, as if under extrasensory control. I agree that it could have been extrasensory to humans, but not to cats. The answer in one word is: Catnip. Carry an opened package of that stuff in your other coat pocket, and all you have to do is sprinkle some of it in the far corner of the room before you even meet the cat that you intend to sensitize. After the cat has been introduced, buttered up and put through its preliminary paces, you tell people that you will "will" it to head for that corner, and sure enough, it will.

As for other "tests" with animals, particularly dogs, there is a sure but simple way of making them become alert or uneasy, as well as to cause them to whine or bark. That is to blow a supersonic whistle, with notes too high for the human ear to hear, but which bring a response from animals. A small whistle, concealed in the mouth, will do the trick perfectly, but there are some people who can get by without one. They

201

practice whistling up the scale until their lips form a note just a trifle above what is audible to people, but will attract the attention of animals. Such supersonic sounds account for the odd behavior of animals on dark nights, or in creaky old houses, things which superstitious folk attribute to ghostly influences.

According to Steiger's book, Olof specializes in ESP tests with playing cards, but from the descriptions given, most of them resemble tricks from a magic catalog. Steiger offsets this by stating that magic has been a hobby of his since he was twelve years old and that he is familiar with the basic repertoire of the professional card manipulator; and he says that he is capable of duplicating many of Olof's experiments. That in itself should brand them as the tricks they actually are, but Steiger adds that as a magician, he would be controlling the experiments and would have to rely on marked cards or specially prepared decks. He then admits that the tests were not conducted under the most rigid controls.

Now there are three factors that feature the work of a good closeup card expert. First, he allows you enough options to make you think that you are setting the terms of the trick. Next, he almost always uses ordinary cards, and generally a borrowed pack at that. Finally, when he does employ special cards, he introduces them so neatly and disposes of them so subtly that their presence is never suspected. Not only that, they are capable of baffling other magicians with such methods. So I can see no reason for excluding Olof Jonsson from the card-worker category. To stress that, let's analyze one of Olof's "memorable experiments" with some of its variations.

Olof has someone think of a card, using their own pack or a new one. The person then looks through the pack himself and to his amazement, the card is gone. Other people can look through the pack, with the same result. Olof, who has never touched the pack, than causes the card to reappear. Once it was found in somebody's pocket, again, under a chess board set with chessmen, on another occasion, under the cushion of a couch where a lady was seated. Occasionally, it arrives back in the pack and is found there after someone looks through again; but quite often, it does not return at all.

Hence Olof has left a trail of friends, who own packs with one missing card. Presumably, they will never get them back, because according to Brad Steiger, it appears that Olof Jonsson makes each card dematerialize and then rematerialize itself in an incredible demonstration of mind over matter. To account for those that vanished completely, Brad came up with the notion that they might be projected into some other dimension of space. He proposed this theory to Olof, who went along with it to a degree, saying that when he makes a card disappear, he feels that energy has been taken from him. He also noted that he became thirsty when doing such experiments, which made him think that if he drank water, the plasma energy might work better.

But all this science fiction gobbledegook still has its seriocomic relief. One night, when he was achieving "harmony with the Cosmic powers of the Universe," as he himself phrases it, Olof had two cards dematerialize from a group that a girl covered with her hands and then rematerialize by creeping up beneath her bra after she had turned away to wash some dishes.

But before delving into more of these refinements, let's proceed with the analysis of the general effect on the basis of the simple type of card trick which it is.

Actually, the only feature that raises any question of special ability on Olof's part is the matter of selecting the card or cards that are to be used in the trick. Steiger insists that the cards are chosen mentally and at random, without the pack ever leaving the hands of the observers. But his details are sketchy regarding the manner of the choice; and in one important case, the person making the report totally forgot what card had been named for the so-called test. Compared to the investigation of a murder mystery, that would be about the same as a witness forgetting whether the victim had been shot, stabbed, or simply died from a dose of poison.

Now, generally, the selected card must be forced if it is to "disappear" from the pack that the performer does not touch from that point on. There are many ways of doing this without handling the pack. For example, the performer asks someone to name a number between one and ten, the usual reply being "seven." He then remarks, "Cards come in two colors—red and black—so one type must be eliminated. Which do you prefer?" If the person says, "Red," the performer replies, "So we'll eliminate the reds." But if the person says, "Black," the performer responds, "So you want the blacks? All right, we'll use a black card." He then remarks, "There are two black suits, clubs and spades. Again we must eliminate a suit, so name the one you want." Either way, the performer "eliminates" the clubs or decides to "use" the spades. He then reminds the chooser that seven was his number, so the card for this experiment will be the seven of spades.

The reason for this force is that the performer has picked up the pack beforehand and has removed and pocketed the seven of spades. This conforms with Steiger's descrption of a "particularly memorable" demonstration, where a woman reported that "this was my deck of cards, and Olof never touched them." Now since Olof happened to be visiting at the lady's house, it would have been quite easy for him to have had access to the pack beforehand, as that is a common "dodge" employed by many impromptu card workers. It should also be noted that nowhere in the account is there any statement that people first looked through the pack to see if the chosen card was there. Olof simply had people cut the pack into smaller heaps and look through them and discover that the chosen card—whatever it happened to be—was gone. Dematerialized, or course.

Now to top that by having the card return to the pack in rematerialized form, Olof would have to handle the pack himself. When working under reasonably stringent conditions, that would be impossible. That, in turn, would explain why Olof so often dispatches the dematerialized card into some never-never land in the form of "another dimension" from which it never returns. Except, of course on occasions when he could slip the card into someone's pocket and let it be found there.

The business of having someone find that he or she is sitting on the vanished card is a good old standby, too, described in many books on card tricks. You have someone place the pack on a chair or coffee table in front of the seated person, and you invite that person to pick up the pack and look through it. In reaching forward, the person rises slightly without realizing it. If you are standing alongside, it is quite easy to slide the card onto the seat, or even beneath a cushion if one happens to be there. Just have it palmed in readiness for the right moment.

Of course, it would be still easier to sneak the card from the pack long enough in advance to plant it under a set-up chess board or beneath a cushion from which the victim never rises at all.

I'm not saying that Olof Jonsson really does such things; I'm merely claiming that he could do them, because I used to know a magician who did something even better.

His name was Salo Ansbach, and his specialty was teaching card tricks to big businessmen, so that they could amaze their friends and become the life of every party. Ansbach would call on a client and sit patiently by the man's desk until he gained his attention. Then Ansbach would bring out a card case and wheedle his victim into naming a certain card. He would then hand the man the pack and when the man found that his card alone was missing, Ansbach would tell him to unlock the bottom drawer of his desk and look for it. There, deep in the drawer, the dumfounded client would find the missing card.

Ansbach worked that gimmick during the preliminary wait. Under cover of his knee, he would slide the right card through the tiny crack at the top of the locked drawer, then give it a quick flip with his second finger. That sent it so far in that it would generally drop behind some object, or skim into a file of loose papers, so the man really had to hunt for it. Once, Ansbach landed a card in a cigar box that was open about a quarter of an inch; and after the man had taken everything out of the drawer and was fuming that the card simply couldn't be there, Ansbach, knowing that it had to be, suggested that he look in the cigar box. There it was, nestled among the perfectos, and the client just couldn't wait to get his money on the line and have Ansbach explain how the miracle was accomplished.

Let's get back to Olof, or rather, get along to him, for Ansbach was in business long before Olof. In some instances, Olof has reportedly caused the missing card to reappear in the pack while people are still looking through the piles. That, too, is easily explained, if you force the proper card—such as the seven of spades—and have a specially printed card as a secret gimmick.

This card has eight spots, like an eight of spades, but the figure "8" is on only one index corner, while a figure "7" is on the other index corner. The trick card has a standard back, matching a type very commonly used, so the performer has simply to make sure that a pack of that brand is available when wanted. Getting hold of the pack beforehand, he removes both the seven and the eight of spades, putting the trick card in the pack instead. In this case, when forcing the card, he can start by saying, "Give me a number from one to ten—rather high." This makes it almost positive that somebody will think of seven; and if they decide to go one better and call for eight, it will work just as well, perhaps even better. Either way, the performer must remember which end is uppermost when the pack is taken from its case.

Suppose the seven of spades has been forced. If the figure "8" is uppermost, the performer tells the person to run through the pack and find the chosen card. Naturally, he won't find it, because the trick card passes as an eight. But if the figure "7" is uppermost, the performer tells that person to hand the pack directly to someone else, so he can look through the pack first. That automatically reverses the special card, bringing the "8" uppermost. The reason for cutting the pack into small piles is that when different people pick them up to look through them, they naturally turn them sideways, so the ends are not changed. By watching people go through the piles, the performer notes the eight of spades when it passes and can therefore predict the pile in which the vanished seven of spades will reappear. He tells someone to pass that pile to another person, thus reversing it, so the seven automatically shows up. Here, it is wise for the performer to pull the card from the pack and show it with a flourish, enabling him to cover the lowermost spots and index corner with his thumb, so that no one will suspect that the card was once an eight.

If he happens to force the eight of spades instead of the seven, the card can be more fully shown at the climax as only the lower index corner needs to be concealed. Either way, it is easy to switch the fake card for its genuine counterpart, because everyone thinks that the experiment is over. By simply thrusting his hands in his pocket, the performer can leave the fake and bring out the real card, without anyone really noticing the action.

Understand, I am not even hinting that Olof ever used fake cards. I am merely asserting that the same effect can be obtained by using them, thus refuting Steiger's notion that the card is physically disintegrated and later reassembled. Maybe neither of them ever heard of the "Fako Deck" which contains the gimmicked card just described along with many others. But they could have heard of it, because the same house that sells it also held exclusive rights to the production of the ESP cards used in the Duke University tests, which Olof also uses in many of his experiments. If Olof hasn't heard of the miraculous effects that this dealer offers in his comprehensive catalog, Brad certainly should have. If he hasn't, I can only say that he hasn't been keeping up on his magic since the age of twelve. The company regularly sells plenty of goods to teen-age magicians.

I could go on to explain equivalents of nearly all the experiments attributed to Olof's psychic powers, but since I am covering a greater variety of methods throughout this book, there is no reason to limit myself to this one field, especially since Olof's feats have been grossly exaggerated. As a typical case, a Swedish professor dealt a card face down from a pack, and Olof took a pair of dice and rolled one of the cubes so it landed on the card. The die came up with a five and when the card was turned face up, it proved to be a five spot. If anybody else had done that, the simple answer would be "marked cards and loaded dice," but not with Olof.

According to the professor, Olof must have learned the value of the card through clairvoyance and controlled the die through telekinesis. Or, in the parlance used at Duke University, he combined ESP with PK to give a double-barreled illustration of the Psi factor. But I still say it could be a simple trick, even though the professor claimed that the cards and dice were his own. To prove my point, I invited my old friend John Scarne, the famous gambling expert, to duplicate the test for a group of keen observers. Scarne switched their deck for a marked one before they knew what was about to happen; and after the card was dealt, he switched the dice for a loaded pair with the needed numbers under their very noses.

Again, this test of Olof's had a comic sequel. To prove that Olof accomplished the miraculous, the witnesses took a photograph of the face-up card and the single die, exactly as they lay. They did this, of all things, to prove to posterity that Olof had not hypnotized them into thinking that the spots on the die matched those on the card! If they had taken a picture of the card face down, the photograph could have been checked to learn if the back was marked; but they would have had to take an x-ray photo of the die to learn if it was loaded. That just shows how easy it is to steer self-appointed investigators onto a wrong track, or how easily they mislead themselves.

Olof's "miracle," by the way, was a very feeble echo of an old trick called the "Spotter," or "Educated Die," which sold for as low as a dime, but is worth a hundred dollars to any mentalist who knows how to "sell" it. You show a fan of six cards, an ace of diamonds and five spot-cards, then let anybody shuffle and deal them in a face down row. Somebody rolls a die and you count to its number—from one to six— and turn up that card. It proves to be the ace of diamonds. Another shuffle, another deal, another roll, and another hit on the ace. This can be repeated, with never a miss, as often as you want.

Actually, each of the "spot cards" can be shown as an ace of diamonds, because it has only a single spot and a phony index at one corner. When fanned with the real ace at the front, the cards all look like spots, but the performer makes sure they are dealt with those ends toward him, so he can show any card as the ace of diamonds by covering the inner corner with his thumb when he picks it up. By having a set of cards with standard backs, the performer can add them to the top of a borrowed pack and be all set for action. Although the performer handles the cards himself, he does it so openly that there seems no room for trickery; and he lets other people roll any die, thus letting them demonstrate clairvoyant telekinesis.

Summing all this, let me reiterate that I personally favor the use of playing cards in telepathic tests, because many people are so familiar with them that they can visualize any card almost automatically. But with dozens of suitable card tricks on tap, fakery becomes too easy, when so-called ESP tests are limited to playing cards alone. The big reason here is that if the operator fails to force a card or gain the necessary cooperation at the start of some demonstration, he can switch to another test and come back to the original one later. This allows all sorts of leeway, without having people realize it. From the size of Olof's repertoire, as listed in Steiger's book, he is well equipped in that department.

But to attribute the "vanish" of a card from a pack to psychokinesis is not only ludicrous, but should be an insult to anyone's intelligence. Take the trick where a magician allows a card to be selected, and then torn to pieces by a spectator who retains one corner. The magician then burns the remainder to ashes, whereupon the card suddenly and visibly appears between two sheets of glass, fully restored except for the missing corner, which fits perfectly when the astonished spectator personally matches it. That beats anything in Olof's repertoire, yet everybody realizes that it's a trick—not a miracle.

To prove a test valid, Olof should cause cards to dematerialize singly, instead of from a pack or a pile; and preferably, it should fade out gradually, like the fabled Cheshire cat. I'll agree that Olof was getting places when he projected two cards beneath the girl's bra, but it still can't match the card between the sheets of glass. So in the final analysis, why use playing cards at all? Why not make random articles dematerialize in the same mysterious manner? According to Olof, he can, but so far he has managed it only a few times a year; and then it is apt to happen spontaneously. As he described it to Brad Steiger, "Something inside me says, 'Now it will happen!' I will be looking at something, a flower, a vase, a book, and it will disappear. And I feel strangely different at that time."

In Sweden, some folks are still talking about the time Olof made a flower dematerialize, then rematerialize in a friend's home on the other side of town, but Olof admits that the account was a trifle exaggerated. He says he was looking at the flower when he had a strong feeling that it would disappear, and it did. But he didn't know where it had gone until a friend called a few days later and told how a flower had dropped on the middle of a table in their home, right out of nowhere.

I hope that Olof at least knows where *he* is going, for if he comes my way, I'll gladly welcome him with some packs of cards and a committee of experts to pass judgment on his work. If he disappears the cards, we'll have a bouquet in readiness, so he can dematerialize that, too.

NINE

Magicians—Mentalists—Mediums.

Those are the three Ms that combine to spell Mystery where the general public is concerned. So much controversy has raged over their respective merits that it is difficult to tell just where one type of operator leaves off and another takes over. But to anyone fully familiar with the workings of all three, it is plain that the fields are closely merged and must be studied accordingly to gain a proper perspective of the whole.

Of these three, the magicians and the mediums represent the utter extremes. Usually, they are so far apart that it is impossible to reconcile one to the other's viewpoint. Each likes to work under conditions of his own choice, before a receptive audience. Put either in the other's place and no results would be forthcoming. It is really ludicrous to watch some hanky-panky artist put over a few party tricks on an informal

TV show and "explain" that these are methods used by mediums to dupe their victims during spiritualistic seances held under test conditions.

I refer specifically to such schoolboy stunts as pulling a collapsible rod from an inside pocket and extending it to tap someone in the dark, so they will think it is a spirit touch; or lifting a card table, also in the dark, by having two stooges, seated opposite each other, simply hook their thumbs beneath the table edge and provide the needed lift. Such chicanery would be impossible at any seance conducted by capable investigators, as they would search the medium to start and would rule out confederacy by providing their committee and nobody else.

Of course there are mediums who prey upon believers who trust them so implicitly that they can get away with anything. These fakers claim that all their seances are held under "test" conditions and often insist on a cursory search by the few skeptics who may happen to be present. But you can be sure that they will have any needed gimmicks planted where they can get at them, particularly as their seances are generally held on their own premises, or in places to which they have access beforehand. But you won't find such mediums bothering with such trivial phenomena as the mere touch of a spirit hand or the lifting of a table. They will have luminous trumpets floating all about

218

the seance room, with voices speaking from them, and they will top the festivities by materializing full-grown forms that believers will recognize as departed friends and relatives.

When a magician undertakes the exposure of a medium, it is usually a case of an amateur going up against a professional. This is no reflection upon the skill of an experienced magician who occasionally tries to blast the spook racket; it's just that he is out of his orbit. Any good professional magician can handle a heckler in the audience, or a "wise guy" who comes up with a committee that is invited on the stage, because the magician knows his business and the troublemaker doesn't. Similarly, a magician, no matter how good, will usually find himself outwitted when he tackles a professional medium on the latter's home ground. He would have to be a professional medium in his own right to get results.

Frankly, I know of only two professional magicians in America who could be regarded as professional mediums as well. One was Harry Houdini; the other is myself. We both gained that distinction through our extensive, firsthand investigations of spiritistic phenomena, and our standing offers of large cash awards to anyone who could produce manifestations that we could not explain or duplicate.

That last proviso put us in the true "pro"

category, for to do whatever a professional medium could, under the same identical conditions, showed that we knew their business as well as our own. Understand, I am not giving undue credit to Houdini and myself; there were other famous stage magicians who could have qualified on the same terms if they had devoted the necessary time to it, but they never did so.

However, when strictly amateur or semipro magicians try to bait mediums, the result can be even more ridiculous than some of the television one-shots. Along that line, here is a hitherto untold story dating back to the mid-1930s. At that time, I was presenting demonstrations of mentalism at the highest prices per performance ever paid to any mystifier. Since these were chiefly private engagements, before exclusive audiences, comparatively few amateur magicians had seen me in person, particularly in smaller cities. I was widely known in magical circles, however, because of my magazine and newspaper articles exposing fraudulent mediums. Those, while throwing consternation into spiritualistic circles, naturally roused the imitative urge of amateur magicians, who then—as now—felt that they had a proprietary right to any magical effect presented by any famous performer, provided they could buy it through the intermediary of a magical dealer, not because he had a right to it, but because they were incapable of making it themselves.

So they figured that if I could challenge mediums, so could they; and any form of magical trickery was allowable in the process. Now at that time, Harry Blackstone, who was rising to the top rank of American magicians, was featuring the "Vanishing Birdcage," in which he held a squarish cage containing a live canary between his outstretched hands, until, in the twinkling of an eye, it disappeared, bird and all, before the astonished gaze of an entire theater audience. Now the "Birdcage" was not Blackstone's invention; it was created by Buatier de Kolta, who had presented it with great success during his lifetime. It had been further developed by a magician called Del Adelphia, in whose capable hands Blackstone had first seen it.

After Del Adelphia's death, Blackstone had added the "Birdcage" to his repertoire and had provided a few new touches, popularizing it to the point where Camel cigarettes had run full-page advertisements, explaining the secret in full, under the title, "It's Fun to be Fooled, but It's More Fun to Know." That was supposed to convey the message that other brands of cigarettes tried to fool you, but if you smoked Camels, you knew the answers. Anyway, almost any magician except Blackstone would have left the Vanishing Birdcage out of his act. Instead, he made huge blowups of the Camel ads, displayed them in the theater lobbies and added the statement, "Come in and Blackstone will still fool you."

Which he did. Why? Because the Camel ad said that the birdcage collapsed and shot up the magician's sleeve, taking the bird with it. That's just what it did do, but the ad didn't add that it went so far up that Blackstone could let skeptical spectators feel his sleeves, yet find no birdcage there. But after Blackstone went on to another town, people were given a refresher course on how the trick was done, not by reading the Camel ads again, for those had gone in the wastebasket, but by watching local magicians try to vanish mail-order birdcages, thinking that they, too, had the needed skill. But too often, the birdcage remained dangling from the would-be wizard's cuff.

So the few who could do the trick properly had to give it up, until a group of magicians in upstate Pennsylvania had a bright idea. Near the historic town of Ephrata was a summer meeting-ground, where spiritualists flocked to receive messages through visiting mediums. So the magicians went there, with their leader carrying a birdcage between his outstretched hands.

He announced "We're magicians. We've come here to expose fake mediums. They claim they can materialize spirits into something solid and then dematerialize them. All right! To prove it, let's see them start with something solid, like this birdcage. I'm going to dematerialize it right before their eyes, in a split second and in broad daylight. Bring on your mediums, so they can see it happen and then try to duplicate it. If they can't, they'll have to admit they're fakers. We're magicians and we know!"

That naturally caused turmoil at the campground, with skittish believers rushing to cottages to warn the mediums that they were being hounded by magicians. Most of the mediums were even more alarmed when they peeked out and saw the magicians slowly advancing with the man with the birdcage repeating his blatant announcement, for most of the mediums were old-timers who remembered the days when Houdini had tried to drive them out of business. There was just one exception. That was a glib, smooth-spoken operator named Frank Decker, who specialized in spirit trumpet work, under the guidance of a control named Patsy, a long-defunct newsboy who piped his messages in a high-pitched falsetto that could very well have come from Decker instead of the trumpet, since all of Decker's seances were conducted in total darkness, which made ventriloquial effects absurdly easy.

In New York, Decker worked for a set of

wealthy believers and since some of his clients patronized the summer meetings, he naturally went along to make sure that rival mediums didn't snipe off some of his paying customers. Also, to impress his select circle, he had made a few attempts to win the award that I offered through *Science and Invention* magazine for any display of genuine spirit phenomena, but on each occasion, I had successfully duplicated his manifestations. In the course of things, Decker had become well briefed on magicians and their ways, so he was well fixed to handle these small-fry.

In response to believers' pleas of, "Oh, what shall we do? What shall we do?", Decker said calmly, "Stay right here, while I call upon my psychic powers." With that, he walked steadily forward to meet the slowly advancing magicians, while the believers watched, breathless and fearful. They saw the magicians pause when Decker reached them and the confrontation lasted for a few minutes! Then, the challengers, with one accord, turned and walked away, nodding to one another as they went out through the entrance, the man with the birdcage going along with them. By then, Decker had turned and was coming back toward the spiritualists, with a fixed stare, like a man in a trance. He suddenly stopped short, clamped his hand to his forehead and asked, "What happened?"

The breathless believers told him how he had met the invading magicians head on and had sent them on their way, but Decker couldn't remember a thing about it. All he recalled was Patsy's voice, suddenly piping from the void, telling him to walk up boldly to the intruders and let Patsy and other spirits convince them that they should go away. So Decker had simply gone into a trance, as he always did when Patsy took over. He was sure, though, that the magicians would not return to annoy the camp meeting again, for Patsy's voice had said so. Whether the prediction was Decker's or Patsy's, it proved correct. They never came back with their birdcage.

Here was the reason why they didn't. When Decker met the magicians, the first thing he said was, "Listen, fellows. Take it easy. You won't get anywhere working this way."

Then, before they could become too defiant, he added, "You know who I am, don't you?"

That brought stares, some a bit puzzled, until the man with the birdcage voiced the general opinion, "No. Who are you?"

"Don't tell me," returned Decker, in his suavest tone, "that you've never heard of Dunninger."

As the rest went silent, one magician gasped, "You—you mean you're Joe Dunninger—"

"I knew somebody would recognize me,"

interposed Decker, "but don't start getting friendly. That would queer everything. These dopes think I'm one of them. So play it straight, like I'm doing."

"I get it," nodded a magician. "You're working it from the inside."

"That's right," agreed Decker, "and I'm planning a big blow-off. On the last night, we'll have everything—levitations, materializations —that's when I'll need people to come busting in and expose the whole racket. I've been wondering where I could get somebody to help me. Now, I know—"

That really brought an outburst.

"Count on us, Dunninger. We'll be ready when you are."

"That's right, Joe. Say, can we call you Joe?"

"If I bring along some of the books you've written, will you autograph them for me?"

"How will we know when you're ready for the blow-off?"

"Give me your phone number," Decker told the spokesman, "but don't write it out. The dopes will think we're getting too friendly. They're not too dumb for that. So just get going, as if you've won your point, and wait to hear from me."

The spokesman gave the phone number, and the magicians nonchalantly went their way, confident that only Dunninger knew why they went. At the time, only Decker knew, but I found out later; not because I was a mind reader, but because Decker told me all about it, the next time he met me.

In contrast to the extremes, as represented by magicians and mediums, mentalists waver in between. Some rely greatly on magical methods, while others attempt actual tests in ESP. However far the pendulum swings, a capable mentalist will come through with results that a dyed-in-the-wool magician could never touch, because a mentalist plays hunches and realizes how often they may come through, while a magician will still be worrying about new ways of sneaking a rabbit into a derby hat—without realizing that derby hats have become extinct, even though rabbits haven't.

One competent mentalist who leaned heavily to the magical side was Ted Annemann. When working for a small or intimate audience, Annemann was superb, easily the equal of Bert Reese, whom I have mentioned elsewhere, but with this difference: Annemann claimed to be simply an entertainer, which he was, while Reese posed as a genuine psychic, which he wasn't. Annemann's ambition was to perform for larger audiences, so he frequently put on his act at magical conventions, where he invariably created a sensation. After one such affair in New Haven, Connecticut, Annemann took the train back to New York and was sitting in the smoking car when Elmer Ransom, a standardized magician of the old school, came along and sat down beside him.

"Your act was great, Ted," complimented Ransom, "but there is one thing about it that I can't quite understand."

"Like what?" asked Annemann.

"Like the way you take chances," returned Ransom. "I know you have ways of guessing what card somebody took, or what name somebody thought of, but what happens if you miss completely? What do you do then?"

"Why, I just keep on trying—"

"But what good will that do? If it doesn't work, you know it can't work. How can you take such chances? I never would!"

Annemann smiled at that statement; then, realizing that he was dealing with a real old-timer, he decided to become a bit whimsical. In a serious tone, he confided, "You know, Elmer, that's when I do it the hard way. I just close my mind to everything else and concentrate on the answer. I shut my eyes and suddenly it appears, like in letters of fire—"

Annemann shut his eyes to illustrate his point. When he opened them, Ransom was getting up from the seat beside him. Nervously, Ransom said, "I left my suitcase in the other car. I'd better go and see that it's all right. I'll be back later, Ted."

Ransom never did come back. He thought he was dealing with an outright nut. He didn't realize that Annemann was kidding him. Like many old-time magicians, he didn't have a sense of humor. If they had, they would have laughed themselves out of business. Anybody could have told them how funny they looked, standing up there in an obsolete dress suit with claw-hammer tails, pulling a bored bunny out of an old plug hat and acting like it was a miracle.

That goes for some modern magicians, too. I have just been reading the comments of an aspiring magical author, who dismisses the work of famous thought-readers with the facetious comment, "Some performers, after years of practice, amaze even themselves with their ability. They almost believe they read minds." It somehow strikes me that this writer was really speaking of himself. Having seen some of his hanky-panky on TV, I would say that he not only amazes himself with his inability, he almost believes he does real magic, even though the viewers know he doesn't.

He also dismisses the findings of competent, highly intelligent investigators who have conducted exhaustive tests in fully equipped ESP laboratories with the statement, "Brilliant scientists and interested laymen who cannot detect how a magician produces a dove from an empty silk handkerchief or conjures an orange under an inverted teacup are not likely to discover the subtle secrets of a mentalist without long study."

That claim is a masterpiece of self-contradiction. Any brilliant scientist or interested person would naturally acquaint himself with a subject before investigating it. They do that when studying ESP and kindred phenomena, so they would do the same with magic—either of the parlor or stage variety—otherwise they would not be investigators. All they would have to do would be go to the same magic shop or order from the mail-order catalogs which carry all the props and gimmicks which magicians use. In a very short time, they would not only know all about producing doves and oranges, they would be doing such tricks themselves and probably much more effectively than the average magician, including the one who made that statement.

Now those same shops and catalogs also sell so-called mind-reading tricks which are even simpler, as it takes more skill to load an orange under a cup than to call off the names of playing cards by using a pack with marked backs, or identifying articles sealed in envelopes, by using your own envelopes and faking them to start. Yet this same writer cites such methods to prove that magicians are comparable to mentalists, which is ridiculous. A capable mentalist picks up impressions from the minds of the people in the audience through methods ranging from sheer psychology to outright hypnosis. If he exaggerates his ability or makes fantastic claims, he has a valid reason for doing so; namely, to put those minds in a mood where they cooperate more willingly and therefore more effectively. No performer could hope to attain a state of acute perception, either sensory or extrasensory, if he depended on the parlor tricks that are frequently peddled under the exaggerated title of "mental magic."

The writer I have just mentioned should know this well, for according to a blurb of a few years ago, he has written fifteen books for magicians, among them two on mental magic. The first book ran to eleven pages, while the second made it to fifteen, due partly to the inclusion of a card trick. The author stated that he had avoided such tricks in the earlier book, but since many readers pointed out that Dunninger does tests with cards, he decided to include one. The book came out about twenty years ago, when I was appearing regularly on TV, so it is obvious why readers showed such interest.

The card trick was so trivial that it was equally obvious why the author had avoided them, but the pamphlet contained a "magazine test" done with a digest-sized magazine that was so utterly faked that the performer couldn't risk letting it out of his hands at any stage of the presentation. That was bad enough, for the very essence of any mental effect with current magazines or other common objects requires either that they be provided by persons present, or be allowed to lie around afterward, where anyone can look at them. What makes it worse, however, is this: After explaining the trick, the writer added that it could be done with larger magazines and that he had used it with a Manhattan telephone book. Imagine, lugging a five-pound phone book around, instead of borrowing one wherever you happen to be! Or else rigging someone's phone book so palpably that you would have to sneak it away with you, rather than have someone look it over later and learn the trick.

I am making a special point of this because although the writer did not state the fact, the phone-book test happens to be a specialty of mine which I introduced many years before and which no one has ever duplicated. In my presentation, I use a borrowed phone book that anyone is allowed to open wherever he wants and choose a name on either page. That name is found in a sealed envelope which I placed with a committee prior to the test; and the committee may also supply a phone book of their own. On many occasions, I have used a stack of out-of-town directories, from which one may be taken at random, yet the test succeeds as usual.

People have talked so much about that "brain buster," as my telephone-book test is termed, that I have actually been offered top-price engagements on the fame of that one effect alone. Hence, even to mention it in the same breath with the abortive version of the faked magazine test described by the magical pamphleteer, is like comparing a Tiffany diamond in an eighteen-carat setting with a brass ring snatched from an old-time Coney Island merry-go-round. Yet since the writer mentioned me elsewhere in his sixteen-page tome, I feel sure that he had heard of my phone-book demonstration and that I am right in regarding his addendum to the "magazine test" as an insinuation that it was the Dunninger method.

All this has a bearing on a subject I have discussed elsewhere, but I will reiterate to give it added emphasis and clarify it further. Often, when talking about such acts as seeing with the fingertips, x-ray vision, and other pretended feats of ESP, I have been asked if I would ever use such methods in my own demonstrations. My answer is double: I not only would, I have— and for two very good reasons.

First, from a long way back, when I was engaged in the investigation of psychic subjects for *Scientific American* and other such publications, I agreed to duplicate or explain any feat of an allegedly supernatural nature, or any so-called spiritistic phenomena. This was exactly what Houdini offered to do when he and I were conducting parallel psychic investigations. We both lived up to that promise in individual demonstrations.

Second, in extending that guarantee to meet new and changing conditions, I have found it necessary to include the supposed supernormal along with the pretended supernatural. Houdini encountered this to some degree and acted accordingly, but fake mediums were still rampant at the time of his death, and it was not until later that self-styled psychics cropped up in numerous other areas, tying in with anything from ESP through witchcraft and on to the outermost reaches of the occult. Now, granting that a feat is advertised as merely supernormal, rather than supernatural, it is still going beyond the sphere of credibility. The effect upon the public is the same, with the insidious factor that one step may lead to the other, so that any fakery in the field of the supernormal, if not flagged at the outset, can graduate into the supernatural class, thus stirring up a whole flock of new fanatics to support it as genuine.

So if someone backs an act with false claims of any description, I have no other choice but to duplicate it. If I should try to accomplish the same effect genuinely, I would not be duplicating the phoney performance. So no matter how boldly or how baldly fakers put over their sham exhibitions, I have to do it their way, or in some very similar fashion, unless I decide to expose the fraud completely, which I have sometimes done. But as a general rule, any exposure should be reserved exclusively for instances where pretenders to the supernatural are involved; not those who stop with claims of only the supernormal. The situation there is that while one may may be claiming ability in some function as x-ray vision, another may be presenting the identical act as nothing more than legitimate entertainment. Hence he should not be penalized for the faker's fault.

I go still farther in this field. I have continually offered to meet any sensible challenge to do the seemingly impossible. Instead of duplicating or producing some supernormal feat that dupes claim they have seen some self-styled psychics do, I have presented tests of my own choice or creation which they should certainly be able to duplicate if they possess the powers that they claim. Always, too, they have had the option of explaining the things I did, so long as I was still on hand to repeat the tests and prove them to be wrong.

On one occasion, I projected a thought to the editor of a newspaper five hundred miles away. I did the same test with the mayor of a city fifteen hundred miles away. Actually, one was no more difficult than the other, for distance seldom makes a difference in experiments of that sort. When I picked up the thought of a headline that another editor chose for the next day's newspaper, he was only several blocks away, but this was a more delicate proposition, as he might have changed his mind at the last moment, leaving me with the impression of a banner headline that he had been considering only a few seconds earlier. Still, he could have been on the other side of the world, or even out of the world entirely, as telepathic tests have been tried with astronauts during space flights, with results of an evidential sort.

When I predicted that a jury would award exactly $2,750 in a $50,000 lawsuit, I had no idea whose mind the impression came from, for it could have been a mass projection from all the jurors, or for that matter, a precognitive flash of the judge's announcement of the award. But the time when I reported that my car had been stolen and then directed the police along a route that I felt the thief had taken, I could very well have duplicated his thought at every turn. Either that, or I was drawn along the course in some magic fashion, for we came across my car bashed against an elevated pillar; and later, I picked the very house into which the man had fled.

My purpose in citing these experiences is to trace back a mere sixty years and more, to draw a definite analogy between Houdini and myself. Houdini claimed the ability to escape from specified restraints, chiefly regulation handcuffs, shackles, and standard straitjackets. He invited challenges on mutually acceptable terms, such as escaping from a packing box, a safe, or a jail cell. He would take on special challenges, provided they conformed to an accepted pattern. For example, when he agreed to escape from the mouth of a loaded cannon with its time fuse ignited, he specified that he was to be bound with ropes, so actually he was effecting a release from a rope tie, a type of escape which he could accomplish to perfection.

Beyond that, he introduced his own contrivances, most notably a giant milk can and a glass-fronted water-torture cell in which he was submerged upside down; and he considered other formidable devices which he never actually constructed. These were so designed that they could be thoroughly examined by a committee of strangers, under the most exacting conditions, yet Houdini invariably made his escape as scheduled.

Just as Houdini utilized those principles to become a master escapologist, I applied them to become a master mentalist. His marvels were in the realm of the physical; mine involved the mind. You might think that made it harder for Houdini and easier for me, but it was the other way around. I know, because I did an escape act and am thoroughly familiar with all the adjuncts and devices appertaining thereto; whereas Houdini's excursions into the mental field never went beyond the rudimentary stage, and his knowledge of the advanced techniques, particularly in regard to the one-man mental act, were virtually nil.

My various mental challenges have involved the following types: Responding to thought impressions or questions put mentally by members of an audience during a regular demonstration. Regular challenges, such as long-distance tests; or any special challenge conforming to a similar pattern, such as naming tomorrow's headline. Experiments of my own devise, such as the telephone-book test, or naming the total of three numbers in the minds of three different persons.

I should add that there is another category, applicable both to Houdini's escapes and my thought impressions. That can be termed the spontaneous type. On occasions when a new or unfamiliar escape went awry and Houdini was confronted with disaster, he would invariably improvise an alternative measure in response to the emergency. In my turn, I have played hunches that have actually left me startled, as with the jury in the damage suit and my tracing of the stolen car.

As I stated earlier, our careers—Houdini's and my own—followed parallel channels; but we differed as individuals, enough so that when our paths crossed, as they did quite frequently, they were sometimes at cross-purposes. To understand that, you would have to know more about Houdini, as well as the times and circumstances under which he and I met. That deserves a chapter in its own right, so such a chapter follows.

TEN

Nearly everybody has heard of Houdini, but if
you ask anyone to tell you something about him
and what he really did, you will receive a
garbled account that sounds like something out
of fantastic fiction. Houdini's career, far from
being the continuous Napoleonic triumph that
he imagined it to be, and as most people picture
it, was decidedly spasmodic. Fortunately his
initial success enabled him to develop new
projects to replace the old, so although he
experienced a succession of ups and downs,
only the high spots were remembered, and he
successfully bridged the gaps between.

One reason for this was that Houdini was
probably the greatest showman since P.T. Barnum; and in keeping with that, his fame, like
Barnum's, was actually the product of publicity.
Both made claims that were far more extravagant than the goods they delivered, but where
Barnum could jest with his public and openly

declare himself "a humbug," Houdini had to play it straight and pose as the great "I am" throughout, since he was intimating that most of his feats were superhuman, even though he disavowed all claims to the supernatural. His only chance to let down and reveal some of the whimsy in his nature was toward the end of his career, when he introduced some hanky-panky magic into his full evening show. Even then, he was in character, for since he was doing tricks that his audiences had seen other magicians perform, Houdini had to treat them as something trivial that he was including partly for his own amusement, while demonstrating that he, too, possessed all the skill that ordinary tricksters claimed. Otherwise, Houdini would no longer have been Houdini.

Another difference was that Barnum wrote an autobiography, which first appeared when he was forty-five years old, and kept adding chapters to new editions which appeared at intervals over the next thirty years, so that the book was updated almost until the time of Barnum's death. Hence facts pertaining to his career and personality were open to discussion, correction, and confirmation while he was still available. Houdini, in contrast, while a copious writer on magical subjects, never went beyond a projective stage where an autobiography was concerned. His articles recounting his life adventures were largely glorified press notices, while the numerous descriptions of his sensational escapes were generally amplifications of the extravagant playbills that advertised them to begin with. He kept a comprehensive diary, which has never been published, but which established many important dates in his career.

Houdini died unexpectedly at the age of fifty-two, when he was nearing the peak of a new career that might have become his greatest. If he had lived a few years more, he would probably have written and published his autobiography, for he had previously dictated several chapters of such material which had unfortunately been lost, and which he intended to repeat from memory as soon as time allowed. He had, in fact, managed to dictate the details of certain incidents for publication in magazine articles; and he had put a trunk full of notes in safekeeping, all pertaining to methods used in his escapes, saying that they were to be published later. These appeared in book form after his death and give a good insight into his technical methods.

But Houdini's own story remains untold, for the simple reason that of several biographies that have been published, only one or two were written by persons who may have seen Houdini, but never met him; while the rest were the work of writers who never even saw him. Yet the longer they wait to write about him, the more authoritative they seem to regard themselves, perhaps because they have had more time to accumulate irrelevant or exaggerated data, with so few of Houdini's contemporaries still around to ridicule it.

Actually, you had to know Houdini personally to recognize the purposes that motivated him and to understand his moods; not only that, you had to know him well. Similarly, you could not judge his ability as a performer on its own merit alone. Always, Houdini was a challenger; to prove that he was right, he had to prove that somebody else was wrong. He became great when he made a rival look small. He carried that to the point where he completely demolished the competition, which superficially seemed like bad judgment on his part, since it eliminated the factor of contrast, which was so much his stock-in-trade. But there, Houdini was still a jump ahead. By getting rid of the tough adversaries, he cleared the field for a new crop of softies that he could mow down as fast as they sprouted up. As a conservationist, Houdini was one of America's first.

With all that, Houdini could become so paradoxical that you couldn't trust your own judgment in appraising him. Houdini took the attitude that when he was right, anyone who disagreed with him was wrong, automatically. Having proven that point on the major issue, Houdini applied it to minor counts as well, showing that they were wrong on those, because whatever they did must be wrong. But if he decided to violate some of those lesser rules, he had that privilege; for since his main aim was always right, he obviously could do no wrong. What was more, he did this so convincingly that he almost invariably won people to his way of thinking, no matter how illogical it might be. I say "almost," because after he staged the same type of switch a dozen times, you would begin to recognize the technique and be ready for it. Yet at that, you never doubted Houdini's own sincerity. The man he fooled most often and most capably was himself.

All this escaped Houdini's biographers, because they followed the accepted pattern of picturing themselves as the person they were writing about, or trying to translate that person's actions in terms of their own sentiments. It was impossible to do that with Houdini, for he was a law unto himself. So the only clues to his real and remarkable character hinge upon the first-hand reports of people who met him often and were capable of appraising him through their own observations; and did so.

One such person was Sir Arthur Conan
Doyle, with whom Houdini had many discussions on the subject of spiritualism, which
Doyle upheld and Houdini denounced. Apart
from that, they were good friends, and Doyle,
with his great literary ability, came up with this
pointed comment on Houdini:

> A prevailing feature of his character
> was a vanity which was so obvious and
> childish that it became more amusing
> than offensive. . . . When he introduced
> his brother to me, he did it by saying,
> "This is the brother of the great Houdi-
> ni." This without any twinkle of humor
> and in a perfectly natural manner.

That typified Houdini perfectly, but the
comment went much farther than Doyle realized, for Doyle himself eulogized Houdini as a
man of mediumistic ability, believing that
Houdini accomplished his escapes through
supernatural aid. It would probably have
amazed Doyle to learn that the brother whom
Houdini introduced so slightingly not only
knew all of Houdini's secrets, but could and did
perform most of his famous feats. To understand that, we must backtrack to the beginning
of their mutual careers, which was in the summer of 1891, when a seventeen-year-old youth

named Ehrich Weiss decided to become a professional magician and took on his brother Theo, who was two years younger, as an assistant.

Ehrich had read the memoirs of Robert-Houdin, a famous French magician, and promptly adapted Houdin's name for their act. So as the Houdini Brothers, Harry and Theo, they played small dates at neighborhood clubs and halls around New York City and finally booked themselves at Coney Island. Magic was highly popular at that period, with such famous performers as Herrmann and Kellar topping a list of a few dozen other "greats" who toured all parts of the United States with full evening shows playing town halls and theaters.

In New York City, the Eden Musee, noted for its waxwork exhibits, had its own magic theater known as Egyptian Hall, where notable magicians played extended engagements. It was there in 1891 that Buatier de Kolta presented his famous "Vanishing Lady" illusion; and a year later, Professor Powell performed a cremation illusion called "She," taken from a scene in a novel by that name, in which a girl was apparently burned alive. Egyptian Hall continued as a magic theater until 1915, when the Eden Musee was moved to Coney Island. I am not digressing when I mention this, because I was

the last magician who played there, finishing a
run of 104 consecutive weeks, the longest continuous engagement ever filled by a magic show
in New York. Later, I talked to Houdini about it,
and he told me that twenty-five years before, his
great ambition had been to present magic at the
old Eden Musee. He had followed the careers of
all the famous magicians who had played there
and gave me interesting sidelights on those
whom I had never seen. But he never performed
there, because he had become a vaudeville
headliner featuring escapes instead of magic.
Now, by a curious twist of fate, the Eden Musee
had gone to Coney Island, the very place from
where he had dreamed of coming to the Eden
Musee.

Still more oddly, Houdini told me all this
when for the first time in years, he was again
doing a straight magic act. That was at the New
York Hippodrome, in a show called "Everything," in which he was the "Ninth Thing" on a
program that included many more. Even the
mighty Hipp, then regarded as the world's
largest auditorium, owed its origin to Coney
Island, for it was inspired by the success of the
big amusement parks which had opened there
around 1900. The prestige of Luna Park, the
biggest and brightest of Coney's amusement
centers, had enabled its promoters to interest

backers in the Hippodrome project, which achieved immediate popularity with financial returns in proportion to its mammoth size.

So Houdini had been able to bypass the staid old Eden Musee and find himself headlined in a theater that had been totally undreamed of, back in the days when the Houdini Brothers had been playing the seaside honky-tonks at the magnificent salary of $12 a week. Contrasted with the fortunes being made by Herrmann and Kellar, with many other touring magicians showing steady annual profits, the Houdini Brothers were small time indeed; but those were days when humble beginnings were regarded as sure tokens of ultimate success. When the Houdini Brothers were making their debut at Coney's beer halls, the penny arcades were putting in a new attracton called the Kinetoscope, which showed pictures that actually moved and became so popular that some of the arcade owners eventually parlayed their operations into gigantic chains of motion picture theaters. Out in Detroit, an obscure mechanic named Henry Ford was puttering in his spare time with a gasoline buggy that was to become the nucleus of a multibillion dollar automobile empire. While elsewhere, another pair of brothers named Wright were playing around with kites and gliders, fancying that someday they might convert them into a contraption that would actually fly.

I mention this to stress how unsophisticated the public was at the start of Houdini's career, for that was to have a definite bearing on his future, and to a marked degree, on mine. Facing Coney Island audiences was hard schooling, for they were sharp enough to detect some of the older tricks that were common to most magic acts, but Houdini recognized that and knew that if he could give them something that would leave them guessing, they would not only spread the word that the Houdini Brothers had a good act; they would come back to see it again.

A book had just come out called *The Revelations of a Spirit Medium*, delving into all the fakery of the spook racket, which was then at its prime; and Harry, who had read it avidly, was more than half inclined to get into the lucrative game himself, if first he could make a go of magic. So he began looking for spook tricks that could be used on the platform, and he came across one that was just the thing to wow the Coney Island clientele.

It was called the "Trunk and Sack" and was worked by the medium and an assistant. First, the assistant's wrists were tied behind his back; then he was placed in a sack that was knotted at the top. Finally, he was locked inside a trunk, which was covered by a curtained cabinet, as was customary with all spirit manifestations. The medium, after a brief spiel, stepped inside the cabinet, then the curtain was whipped aside and there stood the assistant instead. He invited people to unlock the trunk; when they did, they found the sack still tied with somebody inside it. When the sack was opened, the person proved to be the medium, with his hands bound behind him as the assistant's had been.

The going price for a "Substitution Trunk," as it was later known, was fifty dollars, but the Houdini Brothers picked up a secondhand job for less. Actually, the older and more battered such a trunk was, the less it looked like a magical prop. Always, a committee was invited up on the platform to examine the trunk before and after the rapid-fire switch, but nobody had even a remote chance of finding anything wrong with it.

That was because the trick depended on a special gimmick carried by the assistant, enabling him to open a secret panel in the back. A trick tie was used, enabling him to slide out of the knots and the sack, which was also faked, while the medium was locking the trunk and making his spiel. When the medium stepped into the cabinet, the assistant was ready to pop out; and while he was taking his bow, the medium was going in through the back of the trunk and locking the panel.

Proper stalling on the assistant's part gave the medium time to slide into the faked sack, work his wrists into the trick knots, so he could be found there when the trunk was unlocked and opened. But the stunt wasn't entirely foolproof. At one show, Theo forgot the gimmick, and Harry had to unlock the trunk and let him out. After that, Harry always went in at the start and let Theo wind up there at the finish.

While still at Coney Island, Harry met a girl named Beatrice Rahner and married her. When they went with a circus, Theo dropped out of the act and instead of the Houdini Brothers, it was billed as Harry and Bessie Houdini, featuring the trunk trick under the title of "Metamorphosis," with Harry still going in at the start and Bessie coming out at the finish. Later on, Harry began using gimmicked handcuffs instead of a trick rope-tie, to speed the act as well as facilitate it.

Houdini had always invited members of the audience to tie him with the ropes, so now he let them lock him in handcuffs instead. That raised the question: What if some stranger came up on the stage with a pair of handcuffs of his own and demanded to lock Houdini in those? But Harry foresaw that and first familiarized himself with most makes of handcuffs. At that he had to be careful, because after he got out of the hand- cuffs, Bess had to get into them. So if any cuffs looked too difficult for Bess, Houdini used them as a single act, letting people lock them on him, then retiring to the cabinet and coming out free.

Thus Houdini began to specialize in handcuff escapes. Although this was a novelty to some audiences, it was by no means entirely new. Magicians had been escaping from chains, ropes, and boxes for many years, and when inventors began devising new types of hand- cuffs during the Civil War and the period that followed, a new field automatically opened for escape artists. Handcuffs looked formidable from the audience's standpoint and the fact that lawmen used them to keep dangerous criminals in custody made the odds seem all the worse for any performer who tried to shake off such shackles. Actually, though, the performer had an edge that the average spectator never sus- pected. Handcuffs, unlike padlocks on safes or vaults, did not have individual keys. One stand- ard key would unlock any cuff of its pattern, for the simple reason that this enabled any police officer to handcuff or release a prisoner, provid- ed of course that all used the same type of cuffs.

One of the earliest descriptions of the "Hand- cuff Act" appeared in a book called *New Ideas in Magic,* written W.H.J. Shaw in 1902. It is worth quoting verbatim, as it shows how easily the public of that period could be gulled. Shaw stated:

> This act was first introduced by Joe Godfrey, followed by Louis Paul, and in the last ten years, several performers have introduced the act to good success. To work the act successfully, a person must have some nerve, unlimited gall, and be a good talker. The main secret of the act is in having a set of different handcuff keys. While you can do most of the work with eight or ten keys, it is well to have the full set of forty-five keys. When you get into a town or city, you find out what cuffs the police are using and also find out quietly if there are any special makes of cuffs in the city. Find out all you can and have these keys concealed on your person where you can get your hands to them quickly. The opening of handcuffs, if you are prepared for same, is as easy as putting coal into a stove. I could write several pages on this subject, but have not the space and as you require the keys for the act, it is useless

to take up your time. However, I can furnish you with forty-five keys, and full particulars and pointers for the sum of $15. Address W.H.J. Shaw, St. Louis, Mo.

Assuming this account to be correct, and there is other evidence to that effect, Shaw's reference to "the last ten years" puts it back to 1891, the year when the teen-age Houdini Brothers put on their first magic act. Since Godfrey and Paul were in business then, it is obvious that Houdini did not originate the handcuff act, as most people suppose. In fact, for four years beginning with 1895, there were frequent reports of the Houdinis in a magical journal of the period, but not once were handcuffs mentioned. They were with the Welsh Brothers Circus. They were playing the Clark Street Museum in Chicago. They were reporting good business. They were playing the West with great success.

But not one mention of handcuffs.

Do you want to know why not?

I'll tell you why not. During those lean years of nine-a-day appearances in sideshows and honky-tonks, Houdini was learning more about handcuffs, manacles, and other restraints than anybody ever had before. Unlike Shaw's customers who bought fifteen-dollars worth of keys and waited for spectators to bring up handcuffs that fitted them, Houdini bought every type of handcuff that he could afford and studied them in detail. He was able to open any standard handcuffs and even invented devices to facilitate his work, such as a master key that opened many types, a split key to use with strange or difficult cuffs, and best of all, a special extension rod that he could attach to a key to insert in a lock that could not ordinarily be reached.

It was customary for handcuff kings to "plant" regulation cuffs in the audience for two specific reasons. First, if the performer called for people to bring up handcuffs and nobody had any, the act would naturally fizzle. Second, and worse, if somebody came up with handcuffs that he couldn't open, the performer would be stuck unless he had some of his own available to use instead. There were several ways of dealing with strange or doubtful cuffs. They could be rejected on various pretexts, but the best way was to use them along with the more familiar types, in what seemed a really super-test, where four or more pairs of handcuffs were locked to the performer's wrists and forearms, only to have him shake off the entire lot.

Now, instead of that making it tougher, it made it easier, where the performer was concerned. He had the committee lock his wrists in the familiar cuffs to start, so that with three of those on his wrists, the strange pair, which went on last, was well up his forearms. In his cabinet, he used the right keys to unlock the easy cuffs; then he would get rid of the troublesome pair by simply slipping them over his hands, since the girth of his forearm allowed for that. That was why all handcuff kings—Houdini included—specified that they could be locked in several cuffs at once, provided all were standard patterns, or at least with the right of rejecting any that were not.

There were cuffs, however, that were actually regulation, but had to be treated otherwise. Among those was a type known as the "Bean Giant," which differed from other handcuffs in this way: Where many of the others consisted of two bracelets connected with a link or a chain, the Bean Giants had a solid central block, with a small keyhole in the center and the actual cuffs branching out from each side. Thus other cuffs were flexible enough for the performer to get at the locks with a key, but that was impossible with the Bean Giants, hence there was no way for even an expert escape artist to open them, until Houdini devised his extension key for that purpose.

Both these points, the business of escaping from several handcuffs at once, and the rigid construction of the Bean Giants, have a bearing on what follows, so keep them in mind as we continue. For the moment, however, let's get back to Houdini's reasons for going to such extremes to get out of every possible type of handcuff, as well as other restraints, when he could have limited his act and still have gotten by, the way other performers did.

Ever since Houdini had first read the *Revelations of a Spirit Medium*, he had been eager to try his hand at the game, if only to convince himself that the average citizen could be duped as easily as the author of the book claimed. In fact, his introduction to escape work came when he and his friend Joe Rinn took turns tying each other up with ropes to see if they could release themselves and get back into their bonds the way that mediums were supposed to do. Houdini had also heard about the Davenport Brothers, who traveled extensively throughout Europe and America, featuring a cabinet act, in which they were bound with ropes. Yet, as soon as the doors were closed, bells tambourines, and other articles were flung out through curtained openings. Afterward, the brothers were found still tightly tied, so the assumption was that the manifestations had been accomplished through spirit aid, even though the Davenports never made that claim. But the Davenports would only allow themselves to be tied in a specific manner; otherwise, nothing would happen. Houdini, hoping some day to become a sensation in his own right, obviously felt that if he could free himself from any handcuffs or restraints he might encounter, his reputation would be made.

But while he was trying out escapes as a feature of his magic act, he was also working a coded mind-reading act with Bessie and occasionally putting on spirit seances in regular mediumistic style. This reached its peak when Harry and Bessie took a tour with a medicine show, in 1898, but Houdini soon had all he wanted of the spook racket and decided that it would be better to expose such fakery than go along with it. After the tour finished, he went back to work at the dime museums in the Midwest, where he ran into unexpected luck. Martin Beck, who represented the Orpheum Theatre Circuit, was culling the dime museums for acts and was impressed by Houdini's handcuff work. Beck booked Houdini for the circuit, but told him to drop the magic, except for the trunk trick and to make handcuff challenges his big feature. As publicity, Houdini was to escape from local jail cells along the route, which was easy enough, since jail cells, like handcuffs, had locks that could be opened by anyone who had the right keys and the necessary know-how.

DUNNINGER'S SECRETS

Houdini made a big hit on the Orpheum vaudeville circuit and was booked over the Keith circuit when he returned East, but then bookings ran dry and he decided to head for England, where vaudeville was all the rage and American acts were in demand. In London, an agent named Harry Day booked him at the Alhambra Theatre on the condition that he could escape from handcuffs supplied by Scotland Yard, which he promptly did, as the "darbies" used by the Yard were among the easiest to open. It happened that England already had two brothers named Cirnoc, who were working an escape act of their own and were naturally irked when Houdini moved into the big time ahead of them.

One of the Cirnocs showed up at the Alhambra and challenged Houdini to a test. In the course of things, Houdini brought out a pair of Bean Giants, which Cirnoc had never seen, and let Cirnoc lock him in them. Houdini retired to his cabinet, used the special extension rod already described, and soon came out, free of the Beans. He then told Cirnoc to try them, even giving him the key to see if he could do it faster. Naturally, Cirnoc couldn't get out at all, because not having the special gimmick, he couldn't reach the keyhole.

Cirnoc continued to challenge Houdini on other occasions, but whenever they had a match, Cirnoc was the loser, yet for some stupid reason, he kept coming back for more. Except that maybe Cirnoc's reason wasn't exactly stupid. The whole thing could have been a frame-up between Houdini and Cirnoc, since after all, Cirnoc had nothing to lose. Until Houdini came along, it was easy for a handcuff king to bluff the public by planting enough faked cuffs with stooges in the audience to go through with the act. By doing it the hard way, Houdini made it too difficult for other escape acts to compete with him. So the simplest plan was to wait until Houdini went back to America; then the Cirnocs and others could start all over, even defying Houdini to meet their challenges, since he wouldn't be around to do so.

Only it didn't work out that nicely. Houdini made a trip to Germany and created such a sensation that imitators sprang up, expecting to take over when he left for England, where he was booked for an extended return engagement. Harry cabled his brother Theo to come to Germany on the next boat. When Theo arrived, he was booked in the Olympia Theatre in Magdeburg, under the newly coined name of Hardeen. Billed as the "English Escape Champion," the announcement stated that "as a result of his success in London," he had been "rightfully called Houdini the Second."

Not only had Theo never appeared in Lon-

don, he had never worked a handcuff act anywhere, and he hadn't done the trunk switch for
nearly seven years. But all he needed was a full
set of regulation handcuffs with the necessary
gimmicks, a duplicate substitution trunk, and a
few capable assistants. He was then in business,
filling all the engagements that Houdini
couldn't handle. When both appeared in England, sometimes in opposition to each other,
they had the field pretty well monopolized.
When any rivals did crop up, they were sure to
meet with challengers from the audience, planted there by Houdini or Hardeen. The challengers always brought handcuffs that were so
formidable or so unfamiliar that the would-be
escape kings couldn't afford to take a chance
with them.

So it went for the next three or four years,
until Houdini and Hardeen had played the
British vaudeville circuits to a fare-thee-well, in
the full sense of the term. Audiences became
jaded with the stylized handcuff act, where the
performer spent anywhere from a quarter to half
an hour inside a cabinet, shaking off his shackles. Since he always came out free, where was
the suspense? After you saw one escape king,
you had seen them all, whether his name was
Houdini, Hardeen, Cirnoc, Clempert, Mysto,
Hanco, or Who-have-you.

Houdini had foreseen all that, which proves

how great a showman he really was. In later
years, he spoke and wrote about those early days
when human oddities from the American dime
museums were being foisted on the unsuspecting British public as vaudeville headliners.
There were Strong Men, the Girl Who Couldn't
be Lifted, the Bulletproof Man, and Houdini,
who could escape from anything. He very frankly listed himself with the rest, practically admit-
ting that they were only a notch above the Fire
Eaters, Sword Swallowers, Glass Chewers, and
lesser sideshow freaks. The big difference was
that, in Houdini's mind at least, an Escape King
loomed above all the rest; and he was deter-
mined to be the "One and Only," with the
exception of his brother Hardeen, who was
running opposition against the competition.

To read the extravagant press releases and the
boastful blurbs regarding Houdini's early ex-
ploits in England, you would suppose that the
breathless public stood enthralled at everything
he did, with little else to stir popular interest.
Actually, when Houdini arrived there in 1900,
vaudeville was something of an escape in itself.
The country was still under the rule of staid
Queen Victoria and at the same time tangled in
the throes of the unpopular Boer War. Succes-
sive events, such as the Queen's death, the
conclusion of hostilities, and the coronation of

King Edward VII, had ushered in a more sophisticated era, with more exacting demands in entertainment. Houdini had met these to some degree with escapes from straitjackets, packing boxes, and other restraints, but the peak was obviously past by 1905, otherwise he would have stayed abroad.

Instead, he headed back to the United States, only to find rivals already established there, the most formidable being Robert Cunningham, who billed himself as Cunning, the Jailbreaker and who already had a long series of successful engagements to his credit. Obviously, the first item on Houdini's American agenda was to take care of Cunning by branding him an upstart and an impostor. It didn't matter in the slightest that Cunning had been working in America during most of the five years that Houdini had been away. Probably he had been getting confidential reports from people who had seen Houdini's act in England, thus enabling him to imitate it. The fact that Cunning "knew his cuffs" so well that he could invite challenges, as Houdini did, only made the case against him all the stronger.

Cunning was playing a Brooklyn theater, so Houdini and Hardeen showed up there with the avowed purpose of wrecking the jailbreaker's act. Houdini had recently joined the newly formed Society of American Magicians, whose

members solemnly pledged themselves never to
embarrass a fellow performer, but Houdini
either decided the rule wouldn't apply if he
could prove that Cunning was a faker, or he felt
that he would be keeping his vow if he sat back
and let Hardeen do the dirty work. The result
was a near riot, in which most of the audience
sided with Cunning. When police broke up the
conflict, they arrested Hardeen and took him to
the nearest precinct, where instead of demonstrating his own skill as a jailbreaker, he waited
until Houdini bailed him out. The next day,
Hardeen appeared in a Brooklyn court to answer a charge of disorderly conduct, which the
judge dismissed on the grounds that it looked
more like an advertising scheme.

Now, it would seem obvious that Cunning
came out a winner, for Hardeen unquestionably
provoked the whole affair and if the theater
manager had felt that business had been dam-
aged, he would have appeared in court to press
charges. Apparently the judge assumed that
Cunning had framed the whole thing to boost
the box office and that Hardeen had been hired
as a stooge. Nevertheless, a garbled account of
the affair appeared in the next issue of a magical
magazine, *Mahatma*, stating that Cunning had
refused to put on a pair of common handcuffs
Hardeen had brought up on the stage. That

statement was utterly ridiculous, because Cunning invited people to bring up all types of standard handcuffs, so he would have had no reason to reject Hardeen's.

The account also stated that Cunning was jeered by the audience, which was equally preposterous, because Hardeen wouldn't have gotten into a brawl, unless the audience had been siding with Cunning. Obviously, the *Mahatma* article was prejudiced against Cunning, and nobody had to look very far to find out why. The same issue carried a sizeable running advertisement, with a photograph, proclaiming Harry Houdini as the "King of Handcuffs," even though Cunning was working while Houdini wasn't. The same ad continued regularly until *Mahatma* folded rather suddenly, several months later. The final issue carried an additional half-page ad, announcing a new publication, the *Conjurers' Monthly Magazine,* with Houdini as editor-in-chief. So the Brooklyn story in *Mahatma* was merely a warm-up for things to come. Nobody at the time regarded it as anything more than a sop to please Houdini; and it should have been entirely forgotten. However, nearly sixty-five years later, it was revived in paraphrased form under the dubious head of "documentary evidence" by the author of a new book that was blurbed as the "first definitive biography" of Houdini, despite the fact that at least three others had preceded it over a span of more than forty years.

For a reliable report of the Brooklyn confrontation, it is better to take the firsthand recollections of a man who was on the scene and actually played an unsuspected part in the affair. I refer to Jack Dane, of Baltimore, who worked for various magicians over a period of fifty years, both as an assistant and a builder of illusions and other magical equipment. At the time, he was one of Cunning's assistants, and in later years, he often gave a play-by-play description of that eventful evening.

According to Dane, Cunning was going through his usual act and was rather pleased because three or four strangers had come up on the stage in response to his challenge, all bringing standard handcuffs Cunning was equipped to handle. There was one type which required a turn of the key to lock the cuffs, so Cunning asked for the man's key, tested it and found the cuffs in smooth working order; in fact, a bit too smooth, though he didn't recognize that just then. After examining all the cuffs, Cunning let the owners lock them on his wrists; then he retired to his cabinet, obtained his hidden keys and opened the cuffs—all except that one pair. Even though he had the right key for that make, he could not get it into the lock. Before locking the cuffs on Cunning's wrists, the owner must have switched the original key for a duplicate that had been sawed across the middle, almost all the way through. In turning the key, he continued the twist, which not only locked the cuffs, but broke off the upper portion of the key, leaving the rest embedded in the lock. Cunning was unable to insert his own key. Nor could he remove the broken key-end that had been purposely jammed into the lock to ruin his act.

Cunning came from the cabinet still wearing the cuffs and told the audience that the owner had violated the terms of the challenge. In it, Cunning had specified that he would escape from any regulation handcuffs that had not been altered or tampered with in any manner. He accused the man of having tampered with the cuffs when he locked them; and he demanded that the owner unlock the cuffs to prove otherwise. Naturally, the man couldn't, not even with the good key, which he still had in his possession. Cunning, good showman that he was, ordinarily would have dismissed the committee and concluded his act by ringing down the curtain. Later, by getting free of the fixed cuffs with the aid of his assistants, he could have returned to take a bow.

267

But Cunning didn't have a chance. Right then, according to Dane, Hardeen stood up in the audience, shouted who he was and denounced Cunning as a fraud. He declared that the cuffs were standard—which they actually were—and offered a reward if Cunning continued his act and got free of them, or else admit his claims were false. Houdini was also in the audience, ready to back Hardeen, and who knows what Cunning would have done next if the theater manager hadn't come on stage and gotten into the argument. Either the manager thought it was all part of the act, or was completely sold on Cunning's ability as an escape king. In either case, he offered to bet Hardeen a hundred dollars that Cunning would get free. Hardeen retorted that he would take the bet, and having just returned from England, he began shouting in terms of pounds instead of dollars, which brought a big laugh from the Brooklyn audience.

In the midst of the excitement, Cunning turned to Dane, who was standing beside him, and said, "Jack, get me the half key." Then, shaking his handcuffed wrists toward the audience, he finally gained enough quiet to say that he was going ahead with the act anyway, that all he wanted was extra time, to meet the unfair conditions. Dane, meanwhile, had gotten the "half key," a special gimmick that Cunning used to probe unfamiliar locks. The next thing was to get it to Cunning. In the dressing room, Dane had seen an old coffee cup, so he knocked off the handle, filled the cup with water and dropped the half key in it.

Cunning was almost ready to go back into the cabinet when Dane returned on stage. Being in a sweat, he nodded gladly when Dane asked him if he wanted a drink of water. Since the cup had no handle, Cunning had to take it between his hands like a bowl and as he swallowed the water, he saw the key and took it in his mouth with the last gulp. He shoved the cup back in Dane's hands and shook his head when Jack asked if he wanted more water. Waving his handcuffed wrists, he went back into the cabinet.

What followed was one of those long, suspenseful waits so common with escape acts back in the Brooklyn trolley-dodging days when the longer a vaudeville show lasted, the more the audiences thought they had gotten their money's worth. That, of course, was long before the stagehands unionized and began charging overtime. In those days, they were equally eager to hang around, because they, too, had nowhere else to go. So an escape king usually listened from his cabinet for signs of unrest, before emerging to display the shackles that he had shaken off five, ten, fifteen minutes—or even a half an hour before.

But this night, there was no stalling. Cunning was in there, working with the half key on the basis that the quicker he did it, the bigger hit he would score with a certain two members of the audience, who counted more to him than the two thousand Brooklynites who packed the place. Those two, of course, being Hardeen and Houdini. So Cunning was aiming for a record, only Jack Dane wasn't timing it; he was wondering what Cunning was going to do after the half key failed to work. Would he come up with another challenge, another alibi, another stall, another bet—or what?

While Dane was still wondering, the front curtain of the cabinet began to shake. That meant that Cunning might be struggling, or more probably, that he was coming out. If he did come out, still wearing the handcuffs, he might call for another drink of water. If so, this time, there was nothing that Dane could put in it that would help. Only Cunning didn't come out. When the curtain stopped shaking, what came out was a pair of handcuffs. They slithered from beneath the curtain, glittered in the gleam of the footlights and stopped just short of them.

Was it a stall on Cunning's part? Had he slung out a spare set of cuffs that were stashed in the cabinet, to make people think he was getting somewhere? If so, what was coming next?

What came next was Cunning. He swept the curtain away and stepped from the cabinet, spreading his freed arms wide, then pointing to the handcuffs by the footlights. And that, according to Jack Dane, was when the riot really began. The half key had worked and the curtain came down with Cunning taking bows, amid wild acclaim from the enthusiastic audience, except for those surrounding Hardeen. They stopped their cheering to remind him that he had lost his bet, and they wanted to see him pay up, not just a hundred dollars, but a hundred pounds, as he himself had specified, which by the rate of exchange then, was close to five hundred dollars.

Hardeen settled the argument by taking a punch at his loudest-mouthed critic and the fight was on. Theo was a good man in a free-for-all and he had pulled this caper often enough in England to handle it smartly. Still denouncing Cunning as a fraud, and playing the part of an underdog, he gained enough supporters to hold out until the police arrived and took him under their protection. So that was what really happened in Brooklyn, on the night of September 11, 1905.

About the only reliable statement in the *Ma-*

hatma report was its final line, which read, "Ill Harry Houdini was in the audience." That didn't mean that Houdini was feeling sick over what happened. The term "Ill" was an abbreviation for "Illustrious," a title by which members of the Society of American Magicians addressed one another. So it is obvious that whoever wrote the article accepted Houdini's version in preference to Cunning's.

Another of Houdini's brothers, Willie, tried to ruin Cunning's act at a Harlem theater, only a dozen blocks from Houdini's home, but Cunning freed himself by ruining the handcuffs instead. In this case, the cuffs were fixed by dropping bird shot in the ratchets when they were automatically clamped on Cunning's wrists. But Cunning had the necessary tools to pry himself loose, and this time it was Willie who was arrested and booked on charges that were later dismissed.

Other escape artists ran into similar trouble from Houdini, who took the attitude that they had literally stolen his act; and that since he was ready to escape from any regulation irons that they sent up on his stage, they should be ready to escape from any that he sent up on theirs. That was fair enough, but sawed keys and bird shot did not come under the same legitimate head. Knowing Houdini, I would say that he

would have been the first to beef if such tactics
had been tried on him. He was always on the
lookout for strange cuffs that might be used to
get him, and his assistants were trained to gang
up on troublemakers and hustle them off to the
wings and out through the stage door into the
alley, if they became too insistent.

The crux of the matter was that Houdini
wanted the whole field to himself, and not only
did he feel justified in claiming it, his whole
attitude fitted the spirit of those times. That was
the period when trusts, holding companies, and
monopolies were not only tolerated, but ad-
mired. Vaudeville circuits and theater chains
were crowding smaller operators into bankrupt-
cy and blacklisting actors who wouldn't go
along with it. Big city newspapers increased
their circulations by hiring sluggers to beat up
news dealers who sold rival journals. So in
eliminating competition, Houdini was simply
following an accepted pattern. The question
was why he wanted to monopolize the escape
business.

According to one authority on American
vaudeville, Houdini's original aim was to put
out a medicine show, using the handcuff challenge as a big attraction, with jailbreaks forming
a local tie-in. The law required that such a show
carry a bona fide physician, so Houdini staked

his brother Leopold to a medical education "to keep the graft in the family," as the writer bluntly put it. This is reasonably credible, considering that Harry put Theo in business as Hardeen and kept him on call, when needed. But with the rise of vaudeville and the influx of movies, medium shows became obsolete. As vaudeville itself became more sophisticated, handcuff acts were too slow and hackneyed to sustain audience interest.

Even the straitjacket escape, done in full view by both Houdini and Hardeen, was relegated to the status of an outdoor stunt. Packing-box escapes and other challenges were superseded by the giant milk can, which was filled with water and padlocked with the performer inside, so that failure to escape would mean a "drowning death," as the billing put it. Several years later, Houdini topped this with his glass-fronted "Water Torture Cell," where audiences saw him imprisoned upside down, until the curtained cabinet was lowered over it. During the remaining dozen years of his career, the "Upside Down" was practically Houdini's only escape act, except at occasional intervals. Hardeen took on the milk can as his specialty, but he practically retired from the stage, following a Pacific coast tour in 1915, when he played opposition to Houdini, who was working the

Orpheum circuit and booked Hardeen over the Pantages time so they could pose as rivals and crowd out anyone like Cunning.

By then, the era of the "Challenge Handcuff Act" was practically over. As I have already mentioned, Houdini continued with the Water Torture Cell as his one feature escape, and after his death, Hardeen came from retirement, took over Houdini's magic act and revived the milk can to replace the torture cell, continuing with it for nearly twenty years. But there was another reason why Houdini lost interest in handcuffs shortly after World War I; and I was partly responsible for it, as my next chapter will reveal.

ELEVEN

In monopolizing the handcuff act, Houdini was adhering to a fixed policy that having once established a claim, he should never relinquish it—something with which I have always been in full accord. Following World War I, Houdini was planning a series of movie thrillers, starring himself as a master escapist, which might have led to a revival of his handcuff challenges. So the old act still loomed large in his mind.

Understand, there were plenty of magicians who worked handcuffs and other escapes as part of their act. The magic catalogs listed a long line of such items, but that didn't bother Houdini, unless the small-timers began doing escapes over established vaudeville circuits, which would mark them as competition. Houdini made it a practice to cut off such rivals at the source, by preventing their acts from being booked. As a case in point, Herbert Brooks, a skilled card manipulator, at one time closed his act with a fabulous trunk escape that was definitely his own and as fine as anything that Houdini ever did.

That was all the more reason why Houdini couldn't brook Brooks, so to speak. When Brooks signed a contract with the Keith circuit, he had hardly started his tour before Houdini heard about it. Soon, the wheels were in motion, and Brooks was told to cut the trunk escape from his act. He received his full salary, even though he only did half his act and the easier half at that. But he didn't have to be a mind reader to guess who had beefed to the Keith office. Who? Who, as in Houdini.

The same thing applied to me, only I happened to be a mind reader, so the case was somewhat different. I was booked over the Poli time in New England, doing illusions with a company of assistants and the one-man mental act, which I was the first to introduce and which has been so extensively and erroneously copied for the past half century and more. Naturally, I wasn't doing escapes, because I didn't need them, and handcuffs, by then, had become about as "old hat" as the silk "toppers" from which bewhiskered magicians used to produce rabbits, back in the horse-and-carriage days.

However, my mental act created such a sensation that it was only natural that as a mystifier, I should be compared with Houdini, who had played the Keith time with his famous Water Torture Cell, only several months before. Backstage, in one city where I appeared, I was introduced to the chief of the police department, who commented how much he liked my act and casually asked if I did escapes as well. I said that I did and in fact, I prided myself on my knowledge of handcuffs, but seldom worked them because they were identified with Houdini. What was more, I specialized in mental work, which put us in different lines.

"I won't quite go along with that," the chief said with a smile. "If you were working with a combination lock, you might have the edge on Houdini. While he was getting it mechanically, with his keen sense of touch, you could be getting it mentally with that sixth sense of telepathy you talk about."

I gave the nod to that, so he went on, "If you were as good at picking locks as you are at picking minds, I'd still have something that would stump you."

"Like what?" I asked.

"Like the cells in our new jail," said the chief. "When Houdini was here, we offered to challenge him to escape from one of them. He took a look at them and said he would."

"So since Houdini did it, why should I take a try?"

"Because Houdini didn't. He said his publicity had all been set beforehand, so he would come back later. Only he didn't."

I shrugged that off. I was all for Houdini. Why should he bother with a publicity stunt that was already a dead issue? The thing, though, that impressed me, was this. In ninety-nine per cent of the jail escapes, it was the performer—or his press agent—who went to the police with the proposition; not the police who came to him. Often, it has been implied, the advance man carried sufficient "fix" money to assure success beforehand, but I will go on record that Houdini was above all such chicanery.

Again let me emphasize: I knew Houdini.

There were unquestionably times when a certain emolument, honorarium, or payment would prove conducive to cooperation on the part of a high authority. And why not? By the very nature of his office, and his sworn oath to protect the public weal, any jailkeeper from a U.S. marshal down to a mere turnkey, should automatically refuse to go along with anything that would jeopardize or even cast reflection upon his public trust. But if they really felt that way—as indeed, they might—it was always possible to approach the politician who had appointed them to office and arrange the "fix" at that higher level. That took care of it all the way down to the point where it was feasible, but best of all, no fakery was really needed.

You walked in, looked at the jail cell, figured a way to crack it, and went through with the deal. That was it. Sometimes the escape king borrowed a key long enough to get a wax impression of it and make a duplicate. Other times, somebody just jammed a wad of paper into a spring lock, so it wouldn't spring and then gave the high sign to the escape king, as Hardeen once did for Houdini and laughed about it for years afterward. But all that hinged on the assumption that the escape king was the instigator.

So here was the real switch. The police chief, of his own volition, had thrown the thing at Houdini, who wanted none of it, because he didn't need it. Now, he was throwing it at me, and right then, I didn't need it or want it either. But out of courtesy, I went to look at his jail cells, if only to compliment him on their security and suggest that he write to Houdini and ask him please to come back. But in looking them over, I figured just how I could make a nice escape myself. So I asked him if that was what

he wanted and would he publicize it accordingly, to which he said, "Yes."

So I went ahead and did it.

What publicity I got! It spread so fast that a
rush order came from J. J. Murdock, general
manager of the Keith-Albee Vaudeville Exchange, who had booked me over the Poli
circuit, calling for an immediate curtailment of
all such press stunts. By that, I knew that the
press clips must have first reached Harry Houdini in his sanctum sanctorum at 278 West
113th Street and from there rebounded to Murdock's office. I made a long distance call to
Murdock and when he paused for breath between denunciations, I asked if he had checked
the box office returns following the publicity
smash.

He said he hadn't. I suggested that he should.
He said he would. I received a return call,
saying that if I did the same thing at every other
town along the route, he would take care of any
squawks in New York. Really, it was that good.
Only there were no more cities with fine new
jails that had supposedly escape-proof cells and
no more police chiefs who wanted to throw an
honest challenge at a capable performer who
was ready and willing to make a bona fide
escape under seemingly impossible conditions.

So I ended my tour in what I thought was a blaze of glory, only to find that I had walked into trouble.

I had incurred what could have been the undying enmity of the one and only Houdini. I'd known that he was touchy with regard to the Challenge Handcuff Act, which was his stock-in-trade, but I'd figured that his disregard of the jailbreak caper meant that it had become a bygone publicity stunt that was anybody's ball. I knew now why Houdini had been gunning for Cunning over the years, while only taking occasional swipes at lesser rivals in the escape field. It was Cunning's billing as "the Jailbreaker" that marked him as Houdini's top target; and now it looked as though I was slated for the number two spot.

It was through jailbreaks that Houdini had originally sold his handcuff act in vaudeville. All his showbooks and press sheets pictured him running rampant in formidable bastilles, switching surprised prisoners from one cell to another, shucking off shackles and leaving them clanging in his wake. The stuff sounded like the dime novels that were current in those days and the public not only swallowed it wholesale, but turned out to see him defy all comers with his handcuff escapes at the local theater, thus validating the jailbreak of the day before.

Jailbreaks and handcuffs were as suited to the

public taste as corned beef and cabbage, or the icing on a cake. Houdini had made a specialty of escaping from cells that had held notorious criminals, both in America and abroad. In England, he had turned the jailbreaks over to Hardeen, who had booked himself for nearly five years by prefacing his handcuff act with an escape from the local hoosegow, whenever the box office needed a shot in the arm. So by Houdini's reasoning, my debut as a jailbreaker meant that I intended to reactivate the handcuff work that I had occasionally done in the past and turn it into a specialty. Houdini had a way of thinking ahead and being ready for whatever might happen.

It is difficult, now, to trace back this growing animosity, because Houdini never showed it too openly. He was waiting for me to make another move, then it would be his turn to counter. We were moving in different orbits, but we were both in New York much of the time, so we would meet occasionally in magic shops like Martinka's or Hornmann's. It had formerly been, "Hello, Harry," and "Hello, Joe." Now, it was only, "Hello, Harry." That happened only a few times, however, for after that, I did the silent act myself and waited for the cue of "Hello, Joe," to break the freeze. Only the cue never came.

Pretty soon, we were looking for each other,

so we could both turn the other way to study some new trick on the shelf or watch some card workers showing their favorite sleights. We had ways of drifting out, as if we hadn't seen each other, until I decided to call the turn. One day when we were both in Martinka's, I timed my departure to catch up with Houdini on the street, and I put the simple question, "Harry, what's this all about?"

Houdini gave me a quizzical, yet significant look, as if to say, "You should know!" So I picked it up from there, "It goes back to that jail escape I did in New England, doesn't it? You're still peeved about it, aren't you? You're thinking I'll be trying it again and that next I'll be doing a regular handcuff act—that's it, isn't it?"

There are many photographs available of Houdini, showing him in as many moods, some specially posed for theatrical effect, others showing him before, after, or in the midst of an escape. There is even one in which he is speaking behind his hand, as if confiding in the viewer. You can see him as a boy magician or hanging upside down in a straitjacket. You will find all those and many more in books written by people who never knew Houdini, and you can spend a long time comparing such pictures, trying to get an idea of what Houdini was really like.

You'll get nowhere, because there was just one photo that caught the true Houdini, a simple, natural portrait that showed him as himself. It isn't in any of the books just mentioned, but you will find it as a frontispiece in books written by people who really knew him, because they recognized its worth. Study that picture and you will see Houdini as I saw him that day when I demanded a showdown on Sixth Avenue and had to wait for an elevated train to finish rumbling overhead, so I could hear his answer.

Even now, I can almost see the keen glint that came to his eye as he queried, "And suppose that was the case. What then?"

"Then I'll admit I was wrong. Since you claim the handcuff act as your originality, I hadn't any right to move in on it."

"So why didn't you think of that at the time?"

"Because I didn't realize the excitement the jail escape would cause," I replied. "I'm not a fortune-teller, I'm just a mind reader."

Houdini kept his fixed expression, as if challenging me to read his mind and prove it.

"I've been developing my mental act," I continued, "and I wouldn't want anyone to move in on that. Since we see things the same way, you can count me out of the handcuff field entirely."

"Until you change your mind again," Houdini countered. "Then what?"

"I won't change my mind, Harry."

"What proof do I have of that?"

Houdini was showing his real form by then. He had a great way of talking people into writing letters, signing agreements, or making affidavits regarding anything he wanted. Some of the pledges he made his assistants sign, swearing that they would never reveal his secrets, sounded as if they'd been lifted from the pages of *Tom Sawyer* or *Huckleberry Finn*. But when Houdini promised anything, it was usually strictly verbal. You could depend on him to keep his word; he was a stickler for that, but he preferred to let others commit themselves first.

Houdini's request for proof left the burden still on me, so to pull out of the dilemma, I came up with a quick inspiration, something that I'd thought about before, but hadn't intended to broach at this time.

"I wouldn't want to take a chance with a challenge handcuff act," I stated. "Anybody could ruin it. The terms are too liberal."

Houdini gave me a quizzical look that meant to go on.

"You offer to get out of any regulation hand-cuffs," I continued, "and the committee can use two, three, four—any number at one time. Right?"

"Provided they are in working condition," specified Houdini, "and that no one is allowed to tamper with them. We see to that."

By "we," Houdini referred to himself and his assistants, as well as Hardeen and his crew. He naturally didn't include imitators who weren't smart enough to watch for sawed keys or bird shot.

"Bean Giants are regulation," I went on, "but they are tougher than some other types. You can't pick them, and you might have a rough time getting a key into that tiny keyhole in the middle of the big center block."

Anybody but Houdini would have smiled at that; but he knew that I was familiar with the way he had outwitted Cirnoc by using an extension rod to reach the lock with the key. He was sure that there would be a payline coming, but I don't think he had time to guess what it was before I gave it.

"Have you ever wondered," I asked, "just what you would do if somebody locked your wrists in two pairs of Giant Beans, with the keyholes face to face?"

When Houdini jumped to a quick conclusion,

he did it both deliberately and emphatically, as though that settled everything. He came up with one right then, "There would be a way of handling that situation."

"Yes," I agreed, "and about the easiest method would be to have the center block sawed off from both bracelets of one pair so you could unlock the other. But that wouldn't do with a handcuff act."

Naturally, it wouldn't have done at all, as the escape king would be acknowledging himself beaten. It was up to Houdini to come up with an easier way, but the very thought of trying to wedge an extension down between the faced blocks of the two Bean Giants was bad enough, and utilizing a key from that position would be impossible. So Houdini countered with the sharp query, "Have you ever mentioned this to anyone else?"

"Naturally not," I replied. "I didn't think it would be good for the profession."

"It would take some thinking," said Houdini. "Maybe you would do just as well to forget it."

"I'd like to," I agreed, "and I'd like it if you forgot about that jailbreak I did in New England."

Houdini gave a nod that closed the subject. That nod was characteristic. I had seen him give it to somebody who wanted his okay on a

project. It meant for that person to go ahea
his own; if he didn't, he could count u
Houdini to pop up suddenly and ask him w
he hadn't. But in my case, it was strictly in
reverse. It was something that I wasn't to talk
about and if I didn't, he wouldn't. That subject
was handcuffs. To most people, handcuffs were
things of steel. To Houdini, they were lifeblood
—a strange way to put it, but true. Naturally, the
best way to avoid a touchy subject was to talk
about something else. So in our future meetings,
which were fairly frequent, we began immediate discussions of a theme that interested us
both, the investigation of fraudulent spirit mediums.

Our work in that field lay along parallel lines,
but with many links between. Houdini's technique was to bait fake mediums and then
denounce them. My method was to encourage
them and expose them later. As I've mentioned,
Houdini was anxious to cash in on the growing
wave of spiritualism, since he was planning to
put on a big magic show and needed all the spot
publicity and ballyhoo that he could get. I was
younger and planning my career on a long-
range basis, so I could afford to watch how
things developed and play them accordingly.

There was another difference: Houdini, as the
past master of escapes, could outmatch many of

the physical manifestations produced by cabinet mediums, while my mind reading demonstrations far outshone the so-called spirit communications of the sealed message readers, who posed as bona fide clairvoyants. But there were plenty of fakers who played both angles, so both Houdini and I had to be ready for anything and we could each profit by the other's experience.

During one of those casual meetings, Houdini invited me to come to his home and go over matters more in detail. I agreed and Houdini set the time so promptly that I felt sure that he had something very special in mind. In thinking it over, it didn't take me long to decide what it was. Nearly two years before, Houdini had thrown a challenge at John Slater, who made a specialty of appearing at spiritualist conventions and answering questions that were given to him in sealed envelopes. Since the envelopes were gathered beforehand and taken backstage, there were ways of getting at the questions and Slater probably knew most of them, for he had been in the racket so long and so profitably that he was known as the "millionaire medium."

The title was probably deserved, for the meeting where Houdini challenged Slater was held in the old Waldorf Hotel before an audience of more than a thousand who paid three dollars apiece. Since Slater was in similar demand by believers throughout the country, his gains could be calculated by simple arithmetic in those days when the term "income tax" was regarded as an unconfirmed rumor. The point was that Slater, being well heeled with a million dollars more or less, had blandly fluffed off Houdini's offer of $10,000 if Slater could read a sealed question that Houdini handed him.

What was a take of $10,000 from one skeptic, compared to the $150,000 that Slater could take in annually through weekly "pitches" like the Waldorf "lecture" from the very believers that Houdini hoped to unconvince? Slater had given Houdini the brush-off, and from then on had kept clear of New York, rather than risk another confrontation. In fact, it was to take Houdini five years to catch up with Slater at another such meeting, only to have Slater dodge the issue once again. But Slater knew that Houdini was gunning for him; and Houdini, always fore-armed, was checking up on every new development in the field of mentalism, just in case Slater came up with some new method that Houdini couldn't fathom.

Houdini had a wide knowledge of gimmicks, and as perpetual president of the expanding Society of American Magicians, he could depend on informants in every city, who kept him posted on the ways and wiles of local mediums.

In addition, he received full reports on the numerous mind readers who were playing vaudeville circuits, movie houses, and carnivals. But there was one act that had them all guessing —and that act was mine. Even descriptions of it varied, because at that time I was filling private engagements for exclusive groups, and very few qualified magicians ever saw me perform. However, all agreed that at no time did I collect any written questions from the audience; and that frequently I answered unwritten questions in the minds of persons who not only confirmed the fact, but testified that they did not know me and had never seen me before.

Now, Houdini operated on the positive premise that there was a gimmick to everything, no matter how incredible it might seem. He could hardly think otherwise, for without gimmicks, even the simplest of his escapes would have been impossible. Being a man who thought ahead on everything, which accounted for his ability to meet any kind of an emergency, he must have wondered what might happen if a faker like Slater latched onto a method as good as mine. Houdini might have even pictured Slater offering me $10,000 for my "gimmick," knowing he could get it back by simply accepting Houdini's challenge and then going on to amass another million as the one medium

whose communications with the spirit world
could neither be denied nor explained by Houdini.

When I arrived at Houdini's home, my hunch
proved right. His secretary ushered me to his
upstairs office, and Houdini gestured me to a
chair and told me that he would talk with me as
soon as he finished reading some mail. Then he
turned to his secretary and said that if anyone
else called, she should let him know. The
secretary left, Houdini read a few letters, laid
them aside, leaned back with folded arms and
gave me the eye glint as he said, "You were
telling me that you were going in for mind
reading and nothing else."

That was going a good way back, to the time
when we'd had our hassle over the New England jailbreak, so I knew that Bean Giants were
still in Houdini's mind; but that was the nearest
he came to mentioning them. As I nodded, he
added, "I hear you have a good act."

"I work alone," I acknowledged, "and I let
people keep their questions. So it should be
good."

"You could do that with me? Now?"

"Yes, but results vary with different people.
With a full audience, I can choose those who
make the best subjects."

Houdini was shifting some papers on his

desk; and what followed can best be told by
Houdini himself, from his own notes which he
dictated to his secretary, Miss Fiering, shortly
after my visit.

3 o'clock, July 7, 1923.

Dunninger, who has a wonderful
mind reading method, it is stated [sic]
never asked to read any of the papers. I
believe a part of his method is to get a
glimpse of one sentence. He has the
man open up the paper and when it is
opened up, he reads through the light
of the paper.

There were two messages handed to
me in my office. Dunninger sat in front
of me. Before that I was reading some
mail, and I noticed that he was eyeing
my papers, trying to read the contents
of same. That peculiar sixth sense that I
have, made me feel that he was reading
line after line, so much so that it
actually embarrassed me.

I, thereupon turned the papers
around and asked him, "Can you read a
letter upside down?" and he said "No."
I said "a friend of mine at police
headquarters named Cohen could read

letters upside down as fast as he could read them the regulation way." Dunninger said, "That might be very useful."

A short time afterwards, Miss Fiering handed me a note which read, "Just to remind you that Mrs. Padden is downstairs." As I crumpled up the paper to throw it away, Dunninger said, "Think of the signature on that—there is a "J" and a "T"—is that right?" I said, "No, you are wrong." I then recognized the fact that as I was holding it up to read it, he deliberately read through the paper. He could not get the full name because he by accident only saw the J and T of "just to tell." The girl had accidently written both of the words with a capital letter.

A short time afterwards another note was handed to me which read, "There is a young lady waiting to see you in parlor." This time I felt his eye reading through. I purposely held the message so he could not read it, but evidently with his ferrety brown eyes and his vast experience he counted the words and said, "The young lady crosses her Ts very long." All this time he was stalling for time for me to open up the paper wider and I laughed and said, "Yes, she does." Before crumpling up the paper, I challenged him to read what was on it. I could tell by his gaze that the reason he said she makes her Ts with a long cross was that he wanted me to pick up the paper to look at it and to verify his statement. This would enable him to read more of the message. I concealed the writing as much as possible, then crumpled up the paper and Dunninger said, "There are thirteen words on that paper." I said, "I do not know—I will count them." He was positive there were thirteen. Again this was a ruse for me to uncrumple the paper to give him an opportunity for scrutinization. I felt his gaze just as plain as a spray of water. It was piercing and the first gaze I ever met that was solid. He was reaching around corners trying to read. Unfortunately, I counted them out loud and showed him the message. I am sorry I did not let him go ahead so that I could see what his stalls were.

There is no doubt in my mind that he builds up with his interrogation—he is cold and cool and was not nonplussed when I told him what I was doing, and I do not believe that anyone has ever actually detected his method before.

There is no doubt in my mind but that with his abnormal eyesight, his rapidity of reading upside down and through the paper he gets all the information he wants. At least that was the method he used while trying to read the two messages sent in to me.

Dunninger being tall, it is quite easy for him to read over the average human being.

The remarkable part of his eyesight is that the second message was written very faintly. Nevertheless, he was able to count the words and see how the Ts were crossed.

To identify these notes as his own, Houdini wrote his signature at the top of the first page and filed them for future reference. After his untimely death, they were found among his effects and later turned over to me. A copy was also included in the mass of material which he intended for future books. That material was turned over to Houdini's associate, Walter Gibson, who prepared two books from it, *Houdini's*

Escapes and *Houdini's Magic.* In the material, he found the duplicate notes, thus confirming the fact that Houdini regarded those comments as a satisfactory crackdown of my methods.

I definitely recall the incidents mentioned and can state that Houdini's report of the session was one hundred per cent correct except for the explanations, which were one hundred per cent wrong. That is apparent from the discrepancies in the account itself. Houdini says that the first note from his secretary began, "Just to remind you—" but in stating that I somehow spotted the capital letters "J" and "T," he quotes the first three words as "just to tell." Possibly, he meant that the first two words were capitalized, "Just" and "To," so that the note ran "Just To remind you—"; but that made no difference.

Suppose the message was written in two lines:

Just To remind you that
Mrs. Padden is downstairs.

If I had tried to read through the paper—which I didn't—the writing would have been reversed from my viewpoint. In that case, the signature would have been at the lower left instead of the lower right. But the words "Just To" would be at the upper right, ruling them out as signature. Also, the name Mrs. Padden would be at the lower right, so anyone forgetting that the writing was reversed, would be apt to mistake its capitals, "M" and "P," as initials of a signature, rather than the "J" and "T" of "Just To."

Turning the message upside down would bring the words "Just To" into the lower left corner, and if written in old-style script, the letters "J" and "T" would have looked about the same. But the rest of the writing would have been obviously inverted, putting the signature in the upper line instead of the lower. It may seem curious that Houdini would give me such glowing credit for not only reading through the paper but reading upside down as well; and then assume that I would overlook the very fundamentals of such work. That, however, was Houdini's way. When he set his mind on something, that settled it; and he convinced himself so thoroughly that he was able to sell other people on the same idea, no matter how preposterous it might be.

Needless to say, I didn't read through the paper, nor even try to do so. As I recall it, I merely tried to sound Houdini out, because I realized that he wanted to test my ability at answering questions. I mentioned a signature in order to learn whether the note had come from outside or was simply a memo written by his secretary. When Houdini said that I was wrong, I decided that it was probably a memo and when the secretary brought another message on a similar sheet of paper, I was sure of it. Therefore, the secretary had written it and I had already sized her as the precise type who would be apt to emphasize a "t" with a long cross, so I made a comment to that effect. Of course, the "young lady" to whom I referred was Houdini's secretary, not the "young lady" mentioned in the message, as I had no way of reading it.

Using that as a stopgap, I switched to the "word count." This is very effective when worked with the right type of person, and Houdini was literally made to order for it. He, too, had a very precise way and when he first read the message, I figured it for about thirteen words from his eye pauses and a slight motion of his lips. When I mentioned the crossed ts, he ran through it again, enabling me to check my secret count, which Houdini, in his own report, admitted was correct.

Here, another discrepancy should be noted in that report. Houdini said that I called the turn with exactly thirteen words, yet the message contains only eleven. I think that this was due to hurried dictation on Houdini's part, as with the earlier message. The second one probably ran:

There is a young lady
waiting to see you in
the front parlor

That would build the wordage up to the required thirteen; and as I recall the occasion, when I left shortly afterward, Houdini came downstairs with me to see me out the door and then turned toward the front parlor where a young lady was waiting. I presumed that the message had to do with her arrival, but I hadn't read it closely, as Houdini only allowed me a glimpse of it, while counting the total words. Naturally, I didn't even try to read the messages backward through the paper, nor even count the words. If Houdini had openly asked me to "show my stuff" as a mentalist, I would have suggested that he write a question of his own, fold it, and put it in his pocket or seal it in an envelope. Then I would have tried to answer it, as I did with questions in my regular act.

To gain thought impressions, I need full cooperation from persons involved. In writing questions of their own, they automatically concentrate on the words, often forming mental images as well. Random thoughts are not enough, and the two notes handed to Houdini came into that category. In his case, I had a momentary flash that he had told his secretary to hand him a blank slip, so he could trick me into guessing at something that wasn't there. So I decided to sound him out by mentioning a signature rather than a message, thus getting him to commit himself to some degree.

At that time, Houdini had never seen my act, as was evident from the first sentence that he dictated. He had been going on secondhand descriptions, which were probably vague. Very few persons familiar with two-person code acts or old-style message readers were on hand to analyze my work at the private clubs and exclusive parties I was performing at. He knew that I didn't handle or gather questions, so he decided that I had to read them over people's shoulders or through the paper itself. To support the latter theory, he purposely had his desk set at an angle toward the window so that the light from that direction would show through the paper if he held it high enough, which he did with each message after crumpling it as if to throw it away.

I sensed that Houdini was trying to prove something to his own satisfaction, but quite frankly, I never suspected that he thought I was trying to read through the paper. Actually, the light wasn't strong enough for me even to see the writing, let alone read it, so it looked to me as though Houdini had to turn it toward the window so he could read it himself, from his side. But since he had preconvinced himself, he was satisfied with the result and after dictating his report, his next step was to see my act, so as to file the final proof.

That took some time to arrange, but he finally managed it, and here again, I didn't learn the story until after Houdini's death. It came through Houdini's attorney, Bernard Ernst, who was also interested in magic and succeeded Houdini as president of the Society of American Magicians.

Word reached Houdini that I was booked to appear at a prominent New York club, and Houdini recalled that Mr. Ernst was a member there. So Houdini hurriedly contacted him and asked him to make arrangements for Houdini to attend the show.

That proved so easy that it worried Houdini. He decided that if anyone learned that he was going to be there, the news would reach me. In that case, Houdini was sure that I would change my act and switch from answering questions to something else, rather than give him a chance to check my method. So Houdini insisted that his presence be kept a complete secret and to insure that result he said that he would wear a set of false whiskers that he used when he visited parlor mediums whom he intended to expose.

Mr. Ernst assured Houdini that I could not change my act because the entertainment committee of the club had already seen it. He added that the false whiskers would not be needed, because he would arrange for two aisle seats to be kept vacant, about a dozen rows from the front of the house, and that he and Houdini could time their arrival a few minutes before the show began, so that they could take the seats unnoticed.

It worked as planned. The auditorium was filled when the stage lights came on and the house lights dimmed as the master of ceremonies entered from the wing and made a brief opening announcement. Houdini had just arrived at the back of the house and had time to come down the aisle and reach his seat in the semidarkness before the emcee reached the concluding words:

"— and so I have the honor of introducing Dunninger, the Master Mind of Modern Mystery!"

With that, I came on stage, to make my own preliminary speech, in which I stated that I would pass pencils and slips of paper through the audience, along with envelopes in which people could place and keep the questions that they wrote. I usually finished with a gesture that cued the electrician to turn on the house lights, so I could go down the steps into the audience. On this occasion, however, I changed that routine.

There was a burst of welcoming applause, which I normally let subside before I started to speak. This time, I raised my hands, calling for quiet. Then, I said, "I thank you for this welcome, but I feel that tonight, you should reserve your applause for a member of the audience whose name is far greater in the field of mystery than my own. I mean the one and only Harry Houdini!" With that, I gave the cue for the house lights, and as they came on, I added, "He is in the end seat of the twelfth row on my right. Please stand up, Harry, and take a bow."

Houdini took the bow to a tumultuous outburst of applause that enabled him finally to cover his surprise. In fact, I am sure that everyone in the audience, with the exception of Houdini and his companion, Mr. Ernst, supposed that I had been notified that Houdini would be present and just where he would be seated, so that I could handle the introduction exactly as I did. I went right ahead with my show as scheduled, but I did not see Houdini after it was over; and in our later meetings, he did not mention the incident. So it was not until after his death that I learned of the precautions he had planned to escape notice on that occasion, and why he had planned them.

People who heard about it really wondered how I knew that Houdini was in the audience, and I suppose I might have passed it off as genuine mind reading. Perhaps Houdini attributed it in part to what he termed my "abnormal eyesight," which was partly true in this instance, though it went farther than that. From my old Eden Musee days, I had cultivated a habit to which many performers are addicted—that of "counting the house" before I go on stage.

While I was standing in the wing, talking with the master of ceremonies, I was letting my gaze rove over the well-filled auditorium, which was lighted at the time, and those two empty seats immediately caught my eye. To me, any departure from the norm is important at the outset of a show, so when the emcee went out to introduce me, my mind immediately reverted to those seats and I spotted them again, just as the house lights dimmed. There was just enough light for me to see two men arrive there; and one, a hunched figure keeping in the background, made a quick sidle into the aisle seat and eased from sight behind people seated in

DUNNINGER'S SECRETS

the row ahead. It was so characteristic of Houdini that his name instantly flashed to my mind, even though I couldn't have fully recognized him in the gloom. So I played a hunch and it paid off, as so many of my hunches have.

During my act, I distributed slips more widely than usual, inviting people to keep their written questions and put them in envelopes that I tossed out for that purpose. I wanted Houdini to see my act at its very best, so I kept constantly on the go, scarcely pausing at any given spot. I specially distributed an oversized batch of slips in Houdini's own vicinity, giving him a friendly nod as I went by. In picking up thought impressions, I answered questions from all parts of the house, some so far in from the aisles that I couldn't have read them if the writers had deliberately held them up for me to look at.

Yet Houdini still stuck to his notion that I read the questions by getting people to hold them so I could read them through the paper. Since only the house lights were turned on, that would have been impossible, as they furnished no penetrating glare. But to prove his point, Houdini gathered quite a batch of slips that I had given out and added them as samples to the reports that he had dictated earlier.

Now the interesting point was this—those

307

slips, which had my name printed at the top, consisted of a highly opaque paper. When held directly in front of a light, it was impossible to read through any of them. In short, the sample slips, instead of supporting Houdini's claim, completely disproved it; yet he ignored that fact entirely. Or, putting it in reverse, he didn't bother to test the slips because he was sure that he was right to begin with. Therefore, they had to be transparent.

That was Houdini's brand of logic, and it worked to perfection when he dealt with bogus mediums. He could trump up any explanations of how they worked their "miracles," and the only way they could prove that he was wrong was to show how they really did them—and thereby admit that they were frauds. But in trying to explain the methods of legitimate performers like myself, Houdini's guess was no better than anybody else's, and often worse.

Summing it simply: Houdini, in claiming to know everything, was continually and deliberately leading with his chin. To offset that, he never pressed a challenge nor continued a controversy unless he was sure that he held the upper hand. For beneath his pose of an absolute skeptic, Houdini was very much a mystic, who believed that his destiny was as fixed as the stars, even though he belittled astrology along with anything else that pertained to the psychic. Yet in the second paragraph of his dictated report, he speaks of his own "peculiar sixth sense," which he used to probe what was going on in my mind, although he felt that the only way I could tell what was going on in his was by reading upside down and backward.

It should have occurred to him that I might have been using a sixth sense, too. The only difference was that in his case, it didn't work, while in mine, it did. Curiously, Houdini gave me credit for remarkable hypnotic power in stating that he "felt" my gaze as plainly as a "spray," and describing it as "piercing" and "solid." That, too, was something of a paradox, because Houdini, during his dime museum days, had seen so many fake hypnotic acts that he utterly refused to believe that there was any such thing as real hypnotism.

As for that "sixth sense," which we both possessed to some degree, Houdini exhibited it when I made my last visit to his home, just before he left for his final tour. He paid me for some stage illusions that I had delivered to his show, and I offered to drive him downtown in my car, but first we stopped for coffee at a little restaurant around the corner. When we left there, Houdini gripped my arm as I was starting the car and said in that earnest tone of his,

"Drive me back to the house. I must go back there!"

I complied and pulled up in front of the brownstone, assuming that Houdini intended to get out and pick up something that he had forgotten. That was one time I didn't read his mind, for he simply stared from the car window, letting his gaze rove to the window of his top floor office and down again to the basement level below the big front door, as though drinking in the entire scene.

Then, with a nod, he said, "That's all, Joe. Let's go." And as I drove away, he turned toward me and added, "I had to have one more look at the old house. That's the last time I will ever see it."

Houdini was right. He never came back to the house again.

TWELVE

From the time I inaugurated my one-man mental act, many years ago, I emphasized that my entire demonstration would be conducted under rigid test conditions, and I have adhered to that practice ever since. Primarily I am an entertainer; therefore, in my regular performances, I established a pattern designed to intrigue the average spectator rather than to confound the more skeptical onlookers, but I took special pains to impress that latter group as well.

In my repertoire, I always included certain tests which later became known as "brain busters," because they utterly nonplussed the keenest observers and were never duplicated by any other performer. I will say also that they far surpassed any ESP tests like those conducted at Duke University or in other parapsychological laboratories, for the simple reason that they were presented under conditions that were conducive to telepathic results. I also had the opportunity to choose the most suitable persons as my subjects at times when their interest was keyed to the utmost. The more skeptical they were, the better I liked it, because once having participated in a test rather than merely witnessing it, they were all the more impressed.

Two of my most successful tests involved predictions. In one, I wrote a name on a sheet of cardboard that was placed in full view with its blank side toward the audience. Then, a skeptical spectator was given an ordinary telephone book and told to open it at random. That done, he circled his hand over either page, finally stopping on a name and number which were verified by other persons. When the cardboard was turned around, it was found to bear that very name.

Originally, I presented the phone book test with a local directory only, but later I elaborated on it by using any number of out-of-town directories that the audience desired, yet the result was always the same. I predicted the right name in every case.

The other was a prediction involving three numbers of three figures each, chosen mentally by three different members of the audience. I had often done this with one person at a time, projecting the impression of a playing card or a three figure number, as well as picking up such a thought from a person's mind. There, however, it was always possible that there was some subtle suggestion on my part or that I actually hypnotized a person into unconsciously whispering the thought he had in mind.

Bizarre though such theories may seem, they cannot be ruled out scientifically, so to eliminate that possibility, I arranged a "triple test," as follows: I had three people each think of a three-figure number, but instead of visualizing them singly, I concentrated on the potential total and wrote that number on a slate. Then I had each person write his number on a smaller slate and when the column was complete, I gave the slate to a fourth person who added up the figures and announced the total. The big slate, when turned up, revealed that exact number, marking it as the combined result of intermingled brain waves projected by three different persons. Inasmuch as they had no chance to meet before the show, none knew the numbers, and there was no possible chance of collusion, since I had divined the total before any of the numbers were written on the small slate.

When amateur magicians heard about these tests, they tried to imitate them, but with very little success. Always, I came up with some new or more convincing version that put me jumps ahead of imitators. With the phone book, they never got beyond the stage of using just one directory—and that had to be fixed beforehand. With the number test, they tried switching figures to get a fake total, which meant that they couldn't let people check them afterward; but when I did the test, I had them verify their own figures at the finish. Always, I met any new requirements or demands that members of a committee might propose.

But when I began appearing on radio and television, the situation changed. Since the same audiences were following the show regularly, I could no longer repeat my "brain busters," no matter how spectacular or effective they might be. Instead, I had to devise new ones, every week, and since I never repeated those, there was no chance to improve them after they were imitated. One dealer in the Midwest began peddling "mental miracles" so utterly ridiculous that they should have been listed as comedy gags, instead. One, for instance, was an imitation of my famous feat of having a person hold an end of a shoestring, while I hold the other and start counting from one to ten, transmitting the exact number which I have in mind.

People hearing of this usually claim that I must tug on the string when I come to the proper number, thus causing the person to respond by saying, "Stop!" But when they see me perform the feat, they are baffled because the string hangs loose throughout the test, so a tug would mean nothing. But that did not nonplus this genius of the Midwest. He claimed that the string was really a thin rubber tube, with a tiny bulb, or "palpitator," on one end and a large bulb on the other, a device which has actually been used as a comedy gag by running the tube under a tablecloth and secretly squeezing the big bulb so the palpitator will make a glass tilt or a dish jump. So when the performer comes to his number, he applies the squeeze and the volunteer assistant, feeling a sudden throb, thinks he has received a telepathic impulse.

Now, very obviously, no capable performer could risk his reputation by working this device with anyone whose intelligence exceeded the moron level. Hence, in intimating that this was "how Dunninger did it," the man who explained it gave me credit for spotting such dimwits in the audience and using them as unwitting stooges in this particular test. He advised his customers to do the same and probably they could have, considering the low caliber of audiences who probably watched their work. But I could hardly have foisted off such a fraud on my clientele.

In the course of my career, I presented this

test with an ordinary shoestring, using among my many volunteer assistants, Thomas A. Edison, the Prince of Wales (later King Edward VIII), and six presidents of the United States. Every one picked up the mental message without any physical clue whatsoever.

Public interest in mentalism soared to fantastic heights immediately following my first radio appearance in 1943 and has maintained its pace ever since. All the competent performers in the field have credited me with paving the way to their success, and in return, I must compliment them on their individual accomplishments, for in every case, their success was gained through originality and by developing their own personalities. Two who are no longer with us, Dr. Jaks and De Mille, are particularly worthy of places in mentalism's Hall of Fame. Among current performers, Dr. David Hoy is an outstanding member of the craft, while The Amazing Randi is coming rapidly to the fore.

But the field has its woes as well. Years ago, a disappointed bandleader, Richard Himber, tried to gain cheap publicity by performing some hackneyed tricks under the guise of mental magic, finally exposing his methods after they failed to baffle any intelligent witnesses. While today, a still greater menace has loomed into the field. I refer to a blatant imposter who has been aping my style, my delivery, my gestures, and my mannerisms, even to the way I wear my glasses. He has stopped short only at using my name, much though he might like to do so, for that would prove the claim that I have against him. Still worse, he has tried to duplicate some of my tests, but having no knowledge whatever of my methods, the results are so palpably fraudulent that it would be better for the profession if he had come to me and frankly asked to be instructed on the correct procedures.

At that, he still could have goofed things, considering that the bulk of his program is made up of items that the average cub scout could acquire from any well-equipped magic shop. Yet this self-appointed "master mind" has the effrontery to appear on television and present such stuff under the guise of "miracles." For a while, competent mentalists could only sit back and let him get away with it, because if they explained his imitation miracles, the public might have confused them with the superior tests that the bona fide mentalists actually performed. But fortunately, the public itself caught up with this interloper in two ways.

First, some of his stunts were so obviously "faked" or "hoked" that spectators themselves caught on and spread the word following the performances. Second, critics, in reviewing the demonstrations, began finding out that other so-called "miracles" were simply taken from dealers' catalogs and hence were anybody's property.

Once such facts became public knowledge, particularly through newspaper articles, there was no further need to hold them back, so here they are. Early in many of his personal appearances, the Mental Marvel brings out a pack of cards, gives it an overhand shuffle and invites a spectator to remove a batch of cards and shuffle them himself. Then, laying the pack aside and pressing his hand to his forehead, the Marvel announces, "In your hand, I see the three of diamonds—so lay it aside; and now, the six of clubs; and now the nine of hearts; and the queen of spades—lay them all aside. Now go on with the two of diamonds; the five of clubs; the eight of hearts; hold it now! I see the jack of spades—lay it aside—and the ace of diamonds!"

That ends it on a note of triumph, with the final card of the batch. Simply wonderful! And wonderfully simple, if you want to try it for yourself. All you need is a stacked deck, arranged in the following sequence from the top down:

A H, 4 S, 7 D, 10 C, K H, 3 S, 6 D, 9 C, Q H, 2 S, 5 D, 8 C, J H, A S, 4 D, 7 C, 10 H, K S, 3 D, 6 C, 9 H, Q S, 2 D, 5 C, 8 H, J S, A D, 4 C, 7 H,

10S, KD, 3C, 6H, 9S, QD, 2C, 5H, 8S, JD, AC, 4H, 7S, 10D, KC, 3H, 6S, 9D, QC, 2H, 5S, 8D, JC.

This is known as the "Si Stebbins set-up" in honor of an old-time card worker who used it in his vaudeville act, back in the early 1900s. Note that the cards run in ascending values of three each, with ace = 1, jack = 11, queen = 12, king = 13, and then beginning again, so that ace follows jack, two follows queen, and three follows king. Note also that the suits run in regular rotation, hearts, spades, diamonds, clubs, throughout.

This will not be noticed, if you spread the cards face up, saying to your victim, "You can see the cards are all well mixed." Then, turning the pack face down, you can pretend to shuffle it by peeling off about half the pack with your left thumb, then throwing the right-hand half on top. Keep doing this time after and you will appear to be shuffling the pack, whereas you are merely cutting it, without disturbing the set-up rotation. Now you spread the pack, preferably behind your back and tell the spectator to "Take out a batch of cards from anywhere—all in a bunch—and shuffle them."

While he is doing that, you cut the pack at the place where he removed the batch and put the bottom portion on the top. Now, all you have to do is glance at what is now the bottom card of the pack and it will tell you where his batch begins. For example, if you see the king of spades there, you call for the three of diamonds; then the six of clubs; and so on. Since the spectator has actually shuffled his batch of cards, he finds them in mixed order, so it appears that you are calling cards at random, as their names come suddenly to your mind. When the person is down to his last card, you name it triumphantly and the job is done.

This trick is actually two hundred years old, dating back to Pinetti's blindfold act, which I have described elsewhere. From the description it would seem foolproof, but I've heard that the Modern Mental Marvel has goofed it on occasion. For one thing, he claims to be an expert card manipulator, so he likes to show off by giving the pack a rapid-fire false shuffle, which not only makes it look like a card trick instead of a mental mystery, but is apt to mix the setup and cause him to miss the calls. For another, he is apt to get careless and keep on calling for cards after the spectator has run out of them.

Here's another of the Marvel's miracles that you can try out for yourself, though it's rather expensive. In one of his TV shows, he displayed a pack of cards face up, to prove they were all different. Then turned it face down and let somebody spread the cards all over a card table. Then the helper spread a newspaper over the cards and was given a knife and told to stab through the paper anywhere, thus impaling a card. That done, he lifted the knife and tore away the paper, keeping the stabbed card face down on the knife blade. The Marvel looked through another pack, picked out the eight of clubs. The spectator tilted the knife point upward, and the impaled card also proved to be the eight of clubs.

That miracle began with a visit to the nearest hobby shop, to buy a deck of "Daisy" cards. This is a brand printed with marked backs which can be read clear across the room, because the backs are decorated with large daisies, which have their petals arranged like the numbers on a clock. A mere glance at the proper daisy will immediately tell you the suit and value of that particular card.

This was the type of pack that the Marvel spread beneath the newspaper. Once a card was stabbed and the paper torn away, he could tell what the card was. So all he had to do was look through an ordinary pack for the duplicate, bring it out and match them up. There are other packs similar to the "Daisy Deck," all readable by the same system and there are probably hundreds of thousands of such packs in circulation, so it would seem that the Marvel was taking a long risk using one on a TV show.

But not so. First, he had to have marks that could be read at a distance, to avoid staring goggle-eyed at the pack; again, when the filmed show was reduced to the size of an average TV screen, the cards looked so small that it was very difficult to recognize the backs, hence nobody was apt to think that they were marked. So if you want to baffle your friends, invest in a "Daisy Deck" and see how it works. Of course, each time you do the trick, you have one less card in the pack, but you can work it perhaps a dozen times, before anyone notices that the pack has become depleted.

Of course, that wouldn't bother the Mighty Marvel, who is supposed to be grossing $300,-000 a year and therefore could afford to throw away a Daisy Deck a day. But to meet test conditions—which every qualified mentalist does—he should insist that the committee bring their own packs. Also, to prove that marked cards are not involved, he should draw a card from *his pack* before the paper is torn from the knife blade to reveal the stabbed card.

If you could do it that way, before a private audience, without having your host's eight-year-old son exclaim, "Oh, Daddy, he's using a Daisy!" you would be fortunate indeed. But you might not be that lucky. Unlike the Mighty Marvel, you can't refuse to work unless they "include the children out," as Sam Goldwyn used to say. So your only hope is to do it legitimately, letting people provide their own packs, which would puzzle the Mighty Marvel himself, if he happened to be around to witness it. Yes, it can be done that way.

In another TV appearance, the MM went groping around the studio blindfolded, using some secret sense to track down a large toy balloon that a spectator was holding on a string. Finally getting his bearings, the MM bore down upon his prey, made a dramatic gesture with a long pin that he carried and stabbed the balloon so perfectly that it went "POW!"—just like that, informing the rapt viewers that another modern miracle had been achieved in the name of science and ESP. Of course the MM wore his own blindfold, because he hadn't asked people to bring their own blindfolds.

His own, when drawn tight, was thin enough to see through, but he didn't waste time letting people try it for themselves. He stalled long enough during the balloon hunt to bow off, blindfold and all, after accomplishing his aim. It never occurred to anyone to ask why this Marvel, who claimed the ability to find tiny objects hidden almost anywhere, needed an inflated balloon as a target when working blind-folded. The reason was, he couldn't see any-thing smaller without his glasses. If he'd worn them under his blindfold, the act would have looked even funnier than it was.

When the Mighty Marvel signed up for a Canadian TV series, he apparently realized that he needed something more spectacular than stunts with stacked decks and toy balloons. So he picked two items that were advertised by magic dealers and teamed them in combination. He had the mayor of Ottawa think of any card in an imaginary pack and hold a pair of school slates which had been shown completely blank. When the slates were separated, the name of the chosen card was found written in chalk on one of the slates. The stunt made such a hit that the MM repeated it with a Canadian newspaper-man, who thought of three initials, which in due course appeared between the blank slates. He did it again, with the director of a museum, naming an artifact which had been brought to the studio in a sealed box.

This had the critics so agog, that they went to Allen Spraggett of Toronto, who was regarded as Canada's foremost authority on extrasensory perception. Spraggett was conducting a syndi-cated newspaper column called "The Unex-plained," so they expected him to be overwhelmed by this new phenomenon. But Spraggett had been making it a strict practice to separate the real from the phonies before endorsing anyone in his column. He just reached for a handy magic catalog, thumbed it open to the section on "Mental and Spirit Tricks" and pointed out the items that explained the whole thing.

First was the *Ultra Perfect Clipboard, price $35.*

"It's a trick clipboard," Spraggett explained. "The performer asks his guest to write down his secret on a single sheet of paper on the board. The guest takes the paper, leaving only the clipboard behind and says nothing. What he doesn't know is that the hard top of the clipboard is carboned. You peel the top back to see a copy of what was written. The performer has the answer before he goes on stage."

Until Allen Spraggett blew the whistle on the Mighty Marvel, none of the critics had even suspected that anything had been written by the TV guests before the show began. Now, a prompt checkback with the participants proved that Spraggett was right. The Mighty Marvel had suggested that each guest decide upon a thought and write it down; then tear off the slip and keep it without showing it to anyone else. Afterward, the paper could be produced as

evidence against the Mighty Marvel, if he failed
to match the thought.

As the man from the museum put it, "He
handed me an old beat-up clipboard before the
taping began and asked me to write down what
I had brought. I kept the paper with me, though,
so I didn't think anything of it."

Next came the *Deluxe Spirit Slates, price
$8.50.*

Spraggett probably had to dig into an older
catalog to come up with that one, but when he
did, its description fitted the situation to perfection. It ran: "A pair of ordinary school slates are
exhibited showing all four sides. The slates are
placed together and almost immediately there-
after a message written in real chalk will be
found on the slates. A very clever routine for
stage."

Read that over carefully and you will see how
far back it really goes. Probably no schools were
using slates since the early 1900s, and today, if
you can find even one ordinary slate in good
condition, you will have a real collector's item.
So our Mighty Marvel, recognizing that to a new
generation, the old seems new, dug up a pair of
"Spirit Slates" and called it a modern "miracle." There are various ways of producing such
"spirit" messages, but the most popular is to
write it beforehand on one slate and then cover

the writing with a thin sheet of silicate or stiff cardboard, colored to match the slate.

This device is known as a "flap" and by holding it in place with the thumb, both sides of the prepared slate can be shown blank, finally ending with the flap side upward. The unprepared slate is then placed on top and both are turned over together, so the flap drops to the lower slate. When the slate now uppermost is lifted, the message is revealed on its inner surface, and it can be passed for examination, while the other slate is laid aside, the flap going with it. If the performer is worried that somebody may want to examine both slates, he can invest twenty-five dollars in a pair of "Dr. Q Slates," which have a flap that locks automatically in place until released by pressure on a secret gadget. Such slates can be examined before and after the message is produced.

Another stock item that the Mighty Marvel foisted on his TV audiences as a "miracle" involved a padlock and ten different keys. Committee members tried each key in turn, but only the last one would unlock the padlock. A spectator was then bound with a chain, and the padlock was affixed to hold him helpless. After that, the keys were thoroughly mixed in a bowl while the Mighty Marvel left the studio and called in by telephone, ordering ten spectators to form a line so that each could pick a key from the bowl.

These spectators were numbered from one to ten and nobody knew which had the right key, they were so much alike. But over the phone, the Mighty Marvel designated one person— such as number four—to stand aside and retain his key, while the other nine keys were put in a package that was addressed to someone far away and was turned over to a waiting mailman, who took it away in his mail truck. Obviously, it was going to be tough for the chained victim if the Mighty Marvel had guessed wrong; but he not only hadn't, he couldn't. When he returned to the studio, he never touched the mentally selected key, but let the man who held it try it in the padlock. Though the odds were nine to one against it, the key fitted and the prisoner was released amid tumultuous applause, while the Mighty Marvel took a bow for the miracle that couldn't miss.

Since Allen Spraggett also found that one in a magic dealer's latest catalog, again, his explanation deserves to be quoted verbatim.

Spraggett stated: "It's very simple, actually. The one key that opens the lock is the last one of the bunch that is tried. What it does is trigger a mechanism in the lock which enables all the other keys to open it. The performer can't possibly lose."

DUNNINGER'S SECRETS

In summarizing the Mighty Marvel and his self-styled miracles, Spraggett was quoted as follows: "He uses all the standard gimmicks. He has no ESP power whatsoever and is about as psychic as your average oyster. I believe in the ESP phenomenon and I love it, but I object to it being vulgarized and burlesqued by this performer."

Within a few weeks after Allen Spraggett delivered that scathing denunciation of a would-be imitator, he devoted his entire column in "The Unexplained" to a discourse on the "Old Original," who happened to be myself. Here are some excerpts:

> Remember that master of mystery, Dunninger?
>
> During the 1940s and 1950s he was the biggest name among show-business mind readers. On his network radio program and later on a top-rated weekly television show, he electrified audiences by his apparent ability to probe their innermost thoughts. . . .
>
> Let's recall a typical Dunninger television program in the 1950s.
>
> Dunninger was introduced by the announcer as "the man who does the impossible." He strode from the wings —a tall, imposing figure in a blue serge

suit and maroon tie, with a flowing
mane of gray hair. His presence was
commanding, almost hypnotic in its
effect on the audience.

"Ladies and gentlemen," he intoned
in a resonant voice with an ever-so-
slightly-British accent, "my work here
tonight is legitimate. Yes, I really can
tune in upon your minds, but only if
you help me—only if you concentrate.
I am not psychic. I make no supernatural claims. I depend upon your concentration."

Then Dunninger sat down on a chair
on the stage, removed a small pad from
his right-hand coat pocket and flour-
ished it to show that it was blank. He
wrote on the pad.

"I am receiving an impression from
someone in the studio audience," he
said. "I get the impression of the word
'tiger.' Does that mean anything to
anyone?"

A well-dressed lady arose and acknowledged that it did.

"Madam," said Dunninger in a ringing voice, "we have never spoken to
each other?"

"No," the lady replied firmly.

"You pledge your word of honor we have never met before or prearranged anything?"

"Yes," she replied with feeling.

"Very well. Tell me, what is tiger?"

"It's my maiden name," said the lady.

"And what would the name Greer be?"

"That's my married name."

"And who is Almon?" Dunninger asked.

"My husband."

"And Fern?"

"My daughter."

Dunninger said, "Thank you, madam," and the lady, obviously stunned, sat down amid wild applause.

Consider that description, which Allen Spraggett recalled so vividly and accurately after some twenty years. Then compare it with the current comments regarding the Mighty Marvel, as given earlier. You will see the generation gap between the time when the real left off and the phoney took over.

Although the MM may copy my style, you won't find him duplicating my tests, because none of them appear in catalogs of magic and

331

mentalism. They contain only imitations, which therefore represent the limit of his capacity. You may have fun trying some of the stock items for yourself, but don't call them ESP, the way this joker does. A lot more people are delving into those catalogs since Allen Spraggett publicized them.

They might label you as phoney, too.